100 Steps Towards
a Successful Marriage

Daniel Bowman

PublishAmerica
Baltimore

ISBN: 978-1-4489-5737-8
PUBLISHED BY PUBLISHAMERICA, LLLP
www.publishamerica.com
Baltimore

Printed in the United States of America

Foreword

Taking that first step towards marriage is a big one. There seems to be a hundred and one things to do before the honeymoon. Overall, it seems like the biggest concern is just stepping down the aisle. But it is after the wedding ceremony that you will be taking the most steps. Without careful thought and planning too many couples end up taking steps to the divorce court.

The intent of this book is to have couples take a look at the next hundred steps in their marriage to ensure that it is not only successful, but happy as well. Marriage is rapidly diminishing in importance in many parts of the world. This is probably due to the lack of religious beliefs by many people. For example, after a visit to Sweden, my wife and I found that almost 80 percent of the people there have no religious belief whatsoever. Many people just live together, without thought as to what it really means to be a dedicated couple. And believe me, marriage takes dedication. Marriage is two people living as one, instead of two people living separate lives in the same place. It is too easy for a non-married couple to split when times get tough.

However, by analyzing the steps involved in marriage, one can appreciate the differences each has without getting upset. This is the intent of "100 Steps" ...to show couples how to enjoy one another and also how to plan act and trust one another during difficult times. The book is designed for those who are about to get married as well as for those who are.

This book is a result of the author having been married twice.

Although my first marriage lasted for a lengthy period, it was unsuccessful. My second marriage is still in effect after twenty five years and I personally feel it has been most successful. Not only is the book a reflection of these two marriages, it also results from discussions and observations with many friends and relatives.

100 Steps Towards
a Successful Marriage

Chapter 1
Love & Getting Married

Love is something more than a sexual thing. It is a commitment that is difficult to describe. However, by applying common sense along with unselfishness, one can understand how the commitment of marriage can make true love a wonderful happening. Many persons fall in love…and just as many fall out of love, but love along with marriage can make for a lasting relationship. Marriage requires intimacy which refers to the feeling of being in a close personal association and belonging together. It is a familiar and very close effective connection with one another as a result of entering deeply or closely into a relationship through knowledge and experience. Genuine intimacy in marriage requires respect, dialogue, transparency, vulnerability, fidelity, and patience.

Before the marriage, there are several steps necessary to ensure that the couple gets off on the right foot. First and foremost are elements that involve financial planning. And then we have the planning of the wedding itself. Is it going to be a civil ceremony or a religious one? Who is invited? When and where? Etc., etc.

For those already married, many of these steps will become necessary when your sons and daughters marry. Far too often, the mother of the bride will want her daughter to have the wedding she never had. Oftentimes the excessive expense of the marriage could have been avoided and monies could have been used for setting up living facilities for the newlyweds. Fathers can be overly critical of the entire procedure and be especially concerned about the expenses. However, several steps should be followed throughout the marriage. It's an excellent plan to review all the steps, especially on your own anniversary.

Step 1—Two as One

When two people think of themselves instead of himself and herself, we have the makings of love. There are some important aspects of love that will be described in the next chapter about religion. This is a subject that most couples believe can be resolved over time, but when one thinks about the subject, it should be resolved at the start. Besides religion, there are other aspects of love that require understanding by one another and should be thought of. Subjects such as pre-nuptials, finances, and even the marriage ceremony require careful planning. And many of the successful aspects of getting married will become useful well into the marriage itself.

More importantly, there should be respect for one another in any relationship. Respect is not shown by violence or infidelity. Two as one also means that you communicate with your partner. Communicating also means that you listen as well. Hearing the words "I love you" from your spouse or significant other makes you feel good, and gives the sensations of warmth, comfort, and protection. Interestingly, the health benefits of affectionate communication are usually confined to emotionally close relationships, such as marriages, family relationships, and friendships. In close relationships, sharing feelings of love and affection is what makes those relationships special. However, inappropriate affection towards others, such as in an affair, will probably elevate stress rather than reduce it.

Step 2—The Devil Is in the Details

When the hard part of what you are trying to do is in the many small details, you can say, "The devil is in the details." In other words, whatever one does should be done thoroughly; details are important. As such, small things in plans and schemes that are often overlooked, can cause serious problems later on. From the wedding cake, to the reception, to the honeymoon, a couple cannot ignore the plethora of details in each and every step of the wedding. Planning should be a joint effort. My wife and I planned our wedding several months before while vacationing in Jamaica. We wanted to insert some personal thoughts into the ceremony and wrote most of the ceremony while on the beach. We then contacted the pastor of our church to ensure that the parts we wanted inserted into the service were appropriate. If we had waited, we might have found that they weren't, thus changing the emphasis we wanted to make in the ceremony.

Some people also say the *"the devil is in the details"* when they examine a contract of agreement, such as a pre-nuptial. Generally, the agreement looks reasonable at first glance, but a closer examination of the terms and small print may reveal a problem. Couples who sign such an agreement should look it over very carefully, looking for a snag or issue which might ultimately make the deal untenable. The attention to detail is the hallmark of lawyers and accountants and should be read carefully, especially by the bride-to-be.

Looking out for the small details in life is generally a good practice, since it greatly reduces the risk of surprise. While some surprises are pleasant, those planned by the devil are not, so it pays to avoid pitfalls, which are preventable by remembering the important details. Budgeting for the wedding should be determined at the beginning of your plans. *Putting on the Ritz* is not necessary, but having adequate food or refreshments is important. Having an open bar can be quite costly, especially if some of the invited are heavy drinkers. The following steps might seem trivial, but careful planning and application can make your wedding (or the wedding of your son/daughter) a Hollywood performance.

Step 3—The Wedding Dress

A bone of contention in many weddings is the wedding dress. Far too often, the bride-to-be wants an outlandish outfit that is really not becoming and often costs far more than should be spent. The dress should not be too revealing and yet make the bride look desirable. Remember, the wedding is not about a dress. It is about a couple that truly love one another and want the world to know that their love is above reproach.

However, from a historical perspective, weddings during the middle-ages could be a union between families and even countries. Love often had nothing to do with the ceremony. Business or politics was often the driving force between couples, especially among noble or wealthy families. Since the bride represented the wealth and social standing of the family, the dress consisted of expensive fabrics, such as silk, velvet and furs.

Traditionally, wedding dresses are white or some shade of white. This stems from Queen Victoria's wedding in the mid 1600s. Before that time, wedding dresses could be various colors, except for black, which was a sign or mourning, and in some cases red (thought to be a color denoting prostitutes). However, in some Asian countries red is acceptable and preferred. Today in China, white is for the wedding, a red gown for later in the day, and gold for evening.

Thus, the wedding dress can signal a lot about the bride. Accordingly, she is probably better off taking a traditional approach to the wedding attire rather than trying to be overly clever and wearing something brash or daring.

Step 4—The Honeymoon

One of the earliest references to what could be called a honeymoon is in the Old Testament of the Bible, Deuteronomy 24:5 "When a man hath taken a wife, he shall not go out to war, neither shall he be charged with any business; but he shall be free at home and be at home one year, and he shall cheer up the wife he has taken."

In early 19th century England, upper-class couples would often visit relatives who had not been able to attend the wedding. This "bridal tour" was sometimes accompanied by friends or family and the practice soon spread to the rest of Europe. Honeymoons in the modern sense became widespread during the late 19th century until World War I. The most popular honeymoon destinations at the time were the French Riviera and Italy, particularly its seaside resorts and the romantic cities of Rome, Verona and Venice. Typically, honeymoons started on the night the couple was married.

Make the honeymoon something you will always remember. There is actually no set rule as to who pays for the honeymoon. While the bride is deeply involved in the wedding planning, the groom can take the responsibility for planning the honeymoon. This does not mean that he does not ask for her input, but once the two of them decide where to go, the groom is usually responsible for the actual planning and arrangements.

Funding the honeymoon is another matter. Often a couple will fund the honeymoon themselves, especially when parents pick up the tab for the wedding. A couple who can't afford an expensive honeymoon can delay their getaway, take a shorter one than planned, drive instead of fly, or visit a place in the off season to save money. The traditional and customary view that the groom's family pays for the honeymoon comes from a time when a young man about to be married might not yet have money of his own. However, another way to deal with the expense of a honeymoon is having the couple arrange for travel gifts at the appropriate registry. According to the Emily Post Institute, there is no objection from an etiquette point of view for requesting contributions for the honeymoon through a honeymoon registry.

To ensure that your honeymoon trip will be romantic, do all you can to make it even more memorable and add to the romance before you go. This means that if you take care of all the details before the honeymoon, the likelihood is that things will take care of themselves afterwards. More importantly, stay sober for the wedding and honeymoon. There is nothing worse than reading in a newspaper about couples who got involved in a drunken crash or having one member of the party falling off a ship and drowning. Remember, you want to have each moment of your wedding and honeymoon to be pleasant memories.

Delaying the honeymoon is not necessarily recommended, but in some cases it can work out quite well. Our honeymoon was delayed a bit due to our work schedules. However we did take one within six months of our wedding and thoroughly enjoyed it.

Step 5—Respect Yourself

Respect for one's self or for one's own character is a proper regard for and care of one's own person and character. It is important that you should respect yourself. This is especially true for women and should start right at the beginning of your relationship. If you are being mistreated, or your "loved one" is physically abusive, then marriage is not the issue, staying together is. Either get counseling or get out. There is no excuse for abuse. But physical abuse is not the only issue; there are many people who use verbal abuse against their mates, which can be almost as devastating as well.

If you have no self-respect, you can't respect others. At first you think you're just becoming tolerant of others, but you must first become tolerant of yourself before you can turn that outward. This can help you deepen self-respect, provide you with the discipline to have patience in your life and ultimately lead you to the tolerance that allows inner peace. Remember that patience can lead to tolerance.

Step 6—Celebrate Anniversaries

Your wedding anniversary is very important. It is a reminder that the two of you are one. In England and its Commonwealths, one can receive a message from the monarch for 60th, 65th, and 70th wedding anniversaries, and any wedding anniversary after that. This is done by applying to Buckingham Palace in the United Kingdom, or to the Governor-General's office in the other Commonwealths. In Canada, one can also receive a message from the Governor General for 50th and 55th anniversaries.

The situation is similar in Australia, where one can receive a letter of congratulations from the Governor-General on the 50th and all subsequent wedding anniversaries; the Prime Minister, the federal Opposition leader, local members of parliament (both state and federal), and state Governors may also send salutations for the same anniversaries.

In the United States, one can receive a greeting from the President for any wedding anniversary on or after the 50th. Roman Catholics may apply for a Papal blessing through their local diocese for wedding anniversaries of a special nature (25th, 50th, 60th, etc.).

The names of some anniversaries provide guidance for appropriate or traditional gifts for the spouses to give each other or if there is a party these can be appropriate gifts or influence the theme or decoration. These gifts vary in different countries but some years have well-established connections which are now common to most nations, they are—5th Wooden, 10th Tin, 15th Crystal, 20th China, 25th Silver, 30th Pearl, 40th Ruby, 50th Gold, and 60th Diamond.

Originally, the tradition started in medieval Germany when a married couple celebrated their twenty fifth wedding anniversary, the wife was presented by her friends and neighbors with a silver wreath, partly to congratulate them for the good fortune that had prolonged the lives of the couple for so many years and partly in recognition of the fact they must have enjoyed a fairly harmonious relationship. When celebrating a fiftieth anniversary, the wife received a wreath of gold. These anniversaries were known as the silver wedding-day and the golden wedding-day. Over time the number of symbols has expanded and the German tradition was to assign gifts which had direct connections with each stage of married life. The symbols may change over time, for example in the United Kingdom diamond was a well known symbol for the 75th Anniversary but this changed to the now more common 60th anniversary after Queen Victoria's 60 years on the throne was widely marked as her 'Diamond Jubilee'.

Step 7—Tolerance and Patience

Because you are mating another personality with your own, you must exercise tolerance and patience with your partner. It is said by the *Dalai Lama* that the antidotes to hate and anger are tolerance and patience. Therefore the various levels of hate and anger that we experience can be best neutralized by practicing tolerance and patience. Each day we have the opportunity to practice either or both of these qualities. Some days we are better at it than others depending on what else is happening in our lives. Having compassion and empathy for what goes on in another's life is the key to becoming patient and tolerant.

We often lose our patience when reacting to circumstances that seem outside of our control. Of course, the weather is outside of our control as are disasters and accidents. The reaction of being impatient often reveals that there is some underlying factor waiting to be dealt with. Fear is usually the greatest cause of impatient behavior as well as the greatest cause of intolerance.

We are fearful of the unknown, such as finding someone whose beliefs are quite different than our own. It frightens us and we tend to judge them negatively. As such, we do not understand or relate to their situation. We become impatient when there are different points of view instead of embracing that difference and respecting another's opinion. It is their opinion and unless it is being inappropriately forced upon us, then forget it. Agree to disagree and go on being friends or amicable acquaintances.

Having awareness that each person's thoughts, belief system, personal reality is different than the next, provides an avenue for compassion and understanding. Once we remember that where they come from is different than ours, we can embrace that difference. But we must remember that constantly. We have not walked a mile in that person's shoes so we cannot judge why they may act or feel the way they do. Being patient and tolerant is a practice that should extend infinitely within our conscious lives. It even includes being patient and tolerant of those whom we perceive as not being patient and tolerant.

If we are to interact with people who are impatient or intolerant, then we must take the time to observe ourselves to find where we may judge others and have similar reactions in a different setting. Through this practice of self-observation and taking that deep look within, we may allow for more self-tolerance and patience as well as tolerance and patience of others.

Remember that stress creates havoc, and affects our reaction towards others. Learn to not over react when stressed and take the time to meditate, relax, contemplate, pray, eat healthy and enjoy the sunshine and fresh air. One should remember that we are all human beings, and that every day is an opportunity to develop our compassionate nature and to be kind.

Step 8—Fidelity

There are more dimensions to marriage than faithfulness. However without practicing fidelity, marriage can become very difficult, if not impossible, to survive. Combine a good marriage with being aware of and avoiding risks and dangers to the marriage and you have the most powerful tools working in your favor. Although no one can completely prevent the possibility of infidelity, the best cure is always prevention.

Many of the steps for preventing infidelity involve keeping your financial concerns as well as discussions about your marriage private when talking with others…especially with those of the opposite sex.

Make a periodic check on the health of your marriage. Open discussions with your spouse about any issues affecting your relationship with one another are very helpful. However, these discussions should be based on a positive note and not just criticism of one another. And be sure to share information and avoid annoying one another. Likewise spend as much time together doing fun things. Whether this involves going out, watching television or listening to music that you both enjoy, just do it. This cannot only include stepping out several times a week to attend restaurants and entertainment venues, but planning and decorating your home together.

One always has to be aware of the risks that persons of the opposite sex present to a marriage. In particular, avoid being caught in compromising situations involving others of the opposite sex, especially in bars or even staying late at the office. And it is best to not have intimate conversations with others about problems, especially sexual, confronting you and your partner.

Step 9—Divorce

Divorce happens. But unlike the divorce rate of those who married in the 1970s, which is close to 50 percent, the divorce rate of those married more recently is much less, around 43 percent. However, the number of people having children together without marriage has risen. Even though these couples have not married, their custody battles can end up in court as well and can be much more difficult to resolve.

Divorce happened to both my wife and me. However, waiting until the children are grown up is not necessarily the answer. From family to friends, most stated that they did not understand how our first marriages lasted so long. What it amounts to is that if love is gone from the marriage, then something has to be done. Whether or not counseling can resolve the issue, nothing can be resolved unless one faces the issue.

However, importantly is what happens afterwards. Are you and your ex still friends? Can the divorce be resolved peacefully? What happens to the children, property, etc.? If each party requires their own lawyer, expenses can really mount. In some states, divorce rulings are rather cut and dried. Basically, everything is split in half. If both parties work, the two salaries are added together and then split in half. Likewise the length of alimony may be one half the length of the marriage. Thus the need for two attorneys may be moot.

While divorce is quite common today, one forgets it's still emotionally complicated or emotionally devastating. Gone are the days when divorce proceedings focused on dividing the couple's financial assets. Back in the 1960s and 70s, children issues were simplified with the mother getting the children and the father visitation rights. Now it is believed that parenting programs can prevent future problems, such as more litigation. Some 46 states have parent education programs related to divorce with some being mandated. Judges can order parents to attend parenting programs that are aimed at teaching parents to continue parenting together after their marriage or relationship has ended.

Such classes reflect how family law and policy has changed. No longer is the focus on the division of the couple's financial assets. Today, there is more focus on the emotional health of parents as well as the children. And parenting classes vary considerably. To fulfill court orders, there are lecture programs, small discussion groups and a growing number of Internetbased classes that can be used. The basis of many of these programs is to make couples realize that parenting is still necessary and that the children should not have to take on adult roles…let them be children. Basically, a child needs both parents and should not be thrown into the turmoil of the divorce. The biggest asset to maintain in the proceedings and afterwards is courtesy and respect towards one another.

Divorce is a reality in our lives. By taking constructive steps before and during the marriage, divorce can be avoided. First of all, a party lifestyle and the high cost of living often stress families to the breaking point. Alcohol and gambling are also frequent culprits. Likewise if one party has a 9-to-5 job and the other party works a swing or a graveyard shift, divorce rates will be higher. However, if both parties work 9-to-5 jobs, where they see each other in the evenings, divorce rates will be lower.

Instead of arguing over who gets the house, divorcing couples now argue over who is going to take over the debt. Coupled with credit going down the tubes, the possibility of going into foreclosure and who is going to take care of the children, many couples are going to a psychiatrist as well as a lawyer.

Step 10—Last but Not Least—Thank You

From the day you are married there will always be a need to thank someone for something. Right from the start, send out those thank you cards for the gifts, help, and attendance of those involved in your wedding. But sending guests a thank you doesn't stop there; all through your marriage there will be people to thank. Most importantly, remember to thank your partner and especially during those important days like birthdays and anniversaries.

Each and every day provides an opportunity to thank your spouse, children, relatives and friends. A meaningful compliment, especially before a group, is a good way of saying thank you to another person. Periodic small personal gifts or flowers to your spouse can be very rewarding. Likewise, gifts to your children for doing good work in school or around the house become reminders of how much you care for them.

As for other family and friends, remember their anniversaries, Christmas, and other special occasions by sending cards, flowers or gifts. If you can't think of what to send, make a contribution to a charity, church or cause they feel strongly about. Constant communication with a person who is sick or feeling blue is inexpensive, but always greatly appreciated. In today's world there are so many means of communication, telephone, email, letters, texting, etc., that reminding others that you care is so easy and is so appreciated.

Chapter 2
Worship

Since many of you will probably get married in the future or were married in a church, temple, mosque, or civil ceremony, a good starting point is worship. The majority of people in America, and in many others countries, have some level of religious beliefs. It is especially important that a married couple have some common ground in their beliefs. This is not to say that you have to be of the same faith, but I believe it really helps. Far too often, the children will be the ones who suffer, unless the couple has an agreement up front as to what house of worship they will attend. And I firmly believe that your children should participate with you. To me, there is nothing sadder than children without faith.

Step 1—Understand one another's beliefs

When my wife and I first got together, she stated that she was Catholic, while I was a Methodist. As such, she wanted to attend church every Sunday, which was fine with me. However, I didn't think she should have to go alone, so I went with her. Granted, the ceremony was slightly different, but we both used the same bible, so no big deal. As I mentioned before, both of us had been previously married. However, when we wanted to get married, the Catholic Church said an emphatic "No," because of our prior divorce. However, the priest suggested we try the

Episcopal Church down the street. Although, the Episcopal Church is Protestant, its ceremony is almost identical to the Catholic Church. That is what we did and we've been members ever since.

Step 2—Pray together

One of the things that we did, that I believe is very helpful, is to pray together. If one believes in God, then one can pray with another person, no matter what religious affiliation they are with. We always begin our prayers with The Lord's Prayer. Then each of us performs our own little prayer for things that we want blessed or are troubled with. We do this morning and night…together. When I mentioned at a men's discussion group at church that my wife and I prayed together, most were amazed and stated that they never thought of doing something like that. I reminded them that the Lord stated that when two or more meet together in prayer, He is there. I firmly believe He is there when my wife and I pray together.

Prayer is most important and helpful during time of trouble. Whether you are looking for comfort or help with a personal problem, prayer helps you focus. Does praying to God really help? If your demands are excessive, such as asking for a million dollars, the answer is "no," prayer is probably not going to help you. However, if you are troubled or need guidance, I believe He is listening and He will help. It may not be exactly what you want, but is probably the best for you in the long run.

Step 3—Participate Together

We find that our attending church together is rewarding. When we lived in California we were both Acolytes (altar assistants). Granted, it felt funny at first because most Acolytes are quite young. However, this was at the early service and the church had a hard time finding young people to Acolyte at the early hour. As such, many in the congregation were quite complimentary and it was very uplifting.

Worshiping as a family is also rewarding as it is an opportunity for a family to participate together in a positive way. Far too often, one or more members stays home, while another member goes to church alone. And don't limit your participation together to just church. My wife and I do a lot of things together…from riding our bikes to writing books, we do these things jointly.

Step 4—Celebrate the Holidays

All religions have some kind of Holy Day. Among the holidays we greatly enjoy are Christmas and New Years. We didn't sit around and watch football games when we were first married. We decided to travel and Christmas and New Years was the one of the few times of the year that both of us could take off from work. Our first big travel event was going to Sydney, Australia for Christmas and New Years. To say that we had a great time would be an understatement, we had a fabulous time. Since that time, we have spent many Christmas holidays in other countries. And a big advantage of Christmas travel is learning how others celebrate this time of year. Whenever possible, we would attend church in the country we were visiting and it most rewarding to see that others worship much as we do.

Another holiday period that became special was the 4th of July. Most of my wife's relatives resided in the Boston area, while we lived in California. Our first Christmas in the Boston area was almost a disaster. It snowed, snowed and snowed. For those living in California, our idea of snow is that it is something on the mountain tops. Snow doesn't come to you, you go to it…when you want to. Needless to say, it wasn't until we started having grandkids did we realize that we didn't have to go to Boston in December to celebrate Christmas.

Christmas for young children involves a lot of gifts. In fact, so many that any we brought at Christmas became quite insignificant. Since my wife's son has his birthday on the fourth of July, I suggested we go to Boston during the fourth and as a result, celebrate not only his birthday, but have an early Christmas with the grandkids. Therefore, while we were in Boston, we would take the grandchildren to a shopping center and let them get some things they really wanted. Not only were they thrilled, but they knew who got the gifts for them. And we were really happy because we didn't have to fight holiday travel during the winter.

Step 5—Charity and Public Service

Helping someone else can be quite rewarding. And helping someone else doesn't necessarily require a lot of money. My wife and I did get involved in building a house in the *Habitat for Humanity* program. It was most rewarding to see the family move into their new home.

There are a lot of items that can involve charity and service. From helping at hospitals to mentoring, it is always rewarding to see how help that many consider insignificant can really make the one on the receiving end quite thrilled. And to show that service to others has an important meaning, on April 21, 2009, President Barack Obama signed the Edward M. Kennedy Serve America Act at an elementary school in Washington, DC before many government dignitaries and an audience of nonprofit leaders and national service volunteers.

The Serve America Act reauthorizes and expands national service programs administered by the Corporation for National and Community Service, a federal agency created in 1993. The Corporation engages four million Americans in result-driven service each year, including 75,000 AmeriCorps members, 492,000 Senior Corps volunteers, 1.1 million Learn and Serve America students, and 2.2 million additional community volunteers mobilized and managed through the agency's programs.

One of the provisions of the act is to improve service options for experienced Americans by expanding age and income eligibility for Foster Grandparents and Senior Companions, authorizing a Silver Scholars program. This program allows individuals 55 and older who perform 350 hours of service to receive a $1,000 education award. It also permits individuals age 55 and older to transfer their education award to a child or grandchild.

Step 6—Donations

A tithe is one-tenth part of something, usually paid as a voluntary contribution to support a religious organization. Today, tithes are normally paid in cash, check, or stocks, whereas historically tithes could be paid in kind, such as agricultural products. In Europe, some countries operate a formal process linked to the tax system allowing some churches to assess tithes.

In this day and age, 10 percent tithing is probably out the question for many couples, especially at the beginning of raising a family. Coupled with taxes, buying a home and all the other items required for modern day life, many couples just can't manage this. However, this doesn't mean you shouldn't make a contribution. The main thing is to make it on a consistent basis.

Likewise, there are many small items that you can donate that also make a difference. One such item is donating food for the poor. Our church has a food baskets for the poor program. Every week when we go grocery shopping, we buy something for the food baskets at church. Not only does it help the poor, but it makes us more conscious of their plight.

Step 7—Church Social Functions

Church social functions are usually quite inexpensive, and yet can be entertaining or informative. And not all church functions are for women. Attending a men's group also can really be quite challenging. While in California, I attended the men's group for many years. We met in the evening on a monthly basis. It was pot luck (no women serving guys) and the meals were quite interesting. I became notorious for my baked beans and other individuals for their own specialties.

Although we would have a featured speaker once in a while, usually our best meetings were open discussions about life, marriage and religion. No golf or other sport discussions were allowed. I felt that the camaraderie generated by meeting with other men was most worthwhile.

Churches in Early America started social functions as they were the only social center available and thus could exercise some moral control over their members. In the 1800s, many churches used social functions in addition to their religious services to serve the many immigrants to a growing America. Upon their arrival, most immigrants found themselves detached from their previous social order, comfort, and network. The initial problems and challenges they had to deal with included loneliness, lack of knowledge and information about this country, and lack of organized support and assistance. As strangers in an unfamiliar land, they would turn to one another for help. The church easily became the place where they could meet. Even though the church was a religious institution, it became a social one as well.

While not a major problem in rural America, churches in the larger cities used social programs to enable some control over the morals of its younger members as otherwise there were many too many temptations for them. And as a community center, the church allowed its members an alternative to the many taverns, pool halls and other forms of entertainment.

Even today, the churches allow many functions for all their members—men, women and children. Unfortunately, many parents don't use such facilities for themselves or for their children. Far too many children are plunked down in front of the TV or playing computer games that have no moral values.

Step 8—Religious Schooling

Religious schooling can be quite expensive, but if you have no confidence in your local public school system, it may become a necessity. Since people often hold varying religious and non-religious beliefs, government-sponsored religious education can be a source of conflict. Countries vary widely in whether religious education is allowed in public schools. Those that allow it also vary in the type of education provided.

People oppose religious education in public schools on various grounds. One is that it constitutes a state sponsorship or establishment of whatever religious beliefs are taught. Others feel that children who do not belong to that religion will either feel pressure to conform or will be excluded by their peers. Others argue that religious beliefs have historically socialized people's behavior and morality. They feel that teaching religion in school is important to encourage children to be responsible, spiritually sound adults. When I was young, each Thursday afternoon, students in the third and fourth grades went to the church of their parent's choice for religious instruction. Of course education was also provided through supplementary Sunday school for all grades. Today, allowing children time off for religious education is virtually impossible because most children no longer walk to school, but are bussed.

Some parents believe supplementary religious education is inadequate, and send their children to private religious (parochial) schools, which are usually affiliated with a specific denomination. Many faiths also offer accredited private college and graduate-level religious schools.

Step 9—*Recharging your batteries through retreats*

Retreats are great for getting away from everyday life and observing another point of view. The term **retreat** has several related meanings, all of which have in common the notion of safety or temporarily removing oneself from one's usual environment in order to become immersed in a particular subject matter. A retreat can be taken for reasons related to spirituality, stress, health, lifestyle, or social or ecological concerns. Increasingly, churches and other organizations hold retreats to focus board and staff members on key issues such as strategic planning, enhancing communications, problem-solving and creative thinking.

A retreat can either be a time of solitude or a community experience. Some retreats are held in silence, and others may provide a great deal of conversation, depending on the understanding and accepted practices of the host facility and/or the participant(s). Retreats are often conducted at rural or remote locations, either privately, or at a retreat center such as a monastery. Spiritual retreats allow time for reflection, prayer, or meditation. They are considered essential in Buddhism, and retreats are also popular in many Christian churches, where they are seen as mirroring Christ's forty days in the desert.

In California, I went on a retreat weekend at the Episcopal monastery located in Santa Barbara with a group from the men's club. The facility was located in the foothills and really quite beautiful. There were group discussions as well as time spent alone. No radios blaring, no TVs screaming, just peace and quiet. I truly felt that my batteries were recharged.

Step 10—Don't be a Zealot

Personally, I believe persons should be firm in their religious beliefs. Being firm or having religious zeal is not a bad thing, but when it is combined with actions that hurt others, it is zealotry at its worst. Zealot is a term applied to people so overcome with religious fervor that they act in ways harmful to others. The zealots of the first century were so enflamed by their beliefs, and they acted in such harmful ways, that their zealotry did not serve their Jewish community. This resulted in significant anti-Jewish sentiment and tougher laws for all Jews. Their cry for freedom was muted by their acts of terrorism. Thus, zealot in the oldest sense applied to many people, and it cannot be questioned that zealots used violence in an attempt to gain freedom.

It's great to be strong in your religious beliefs and to have good knowledge about what one stands for. But to insult others who may be weaker in their beliefs and to try to convert them to yours is not wise, unless they are seeking your help. As they say…stay away from arguing about religion and politics.

Chapter 3
Children

Procreation is one aspect of a man and a woman getting together, which should be a blessed event for many couples...and each couple is called to responsible parenthood. Procreation is a vital act because it is the only way by which nature perpetuates our species. Unfortunately many children are unplanned for and many are born to unwed mothers. However, that should not negate a person's responsibility for raising a child to be good. And a good child is not only a joy, but can make you proud as a parent.

There are many advantages to having a good child. Properly brought up, loved, and educated, the child should do well in school. With proper encouragement he/she should end up ahead in this competitive world. Through proper care and guidance your child should be quite successful and happy in life.

Step 1—Planning

Planning for children is not easy, especially in the height of passion. However, even if a pregnancy isn't planned for, planning for the birth and the raising of the child should begin immediately after finding out. Personally, I don't believe abortion is a solution. There are too many negatives involved.

Unfortunately, politicians have entered the fray and now it seems like young dads have no responsibilities. They don't have to marry the girl and it seems like they have little or no financial responsibility. Grandparents with children occurs all too often as young women have babies, only to find out that raising a child takes dedication—mentally, physically, and monetarily. Oftentimes, the young woman's parents or grandparents will end up raising the child, or else the child is given up for adoption.

Step 2—Enjoy your Children

Children should be enjoyed. Granted, they can be demanding, but overall there are many aspects of their being around that make life both enjoyable and rewarding. Watching them grow is a constant reminder of your own childhood, and the difficulties and joys you experienced. Be aware of what your child can and cannot do as children develop at different rates. They have different strengths and weaknesses and when your child misbehaves, it may be that he/she simply cannot do what you are asking or does not understand what you are saying.

Always pay attention to your child's feelings. Watch for times when misbehavior has a pattern, like if your child is feeling jealous. Talk with him/her about this rather than just giving consequences. Spend as much time with your child as you can without being overbearing. Also let them explore life on their own without your undue interference. Equally important, be available to protect, counsel, and console them during difficult times. Babies who are not held, played with, loved, and do not receive attention may fail to grow and can become depressed later on. However, loving, hugging, interacting and playing with your children will have a strong effect on their overall development. Last but not least, show your children that you love them and that their best interests are also your own. The loving connection formed between you and your children along with your one-on-one interaction can provide the foundation for their higher thinking skills.

Step 3—Schooling

Usually we think of schooling as a stage in life that comes after the child is four or five. Education in its broadest sense is any act or experience that has a formative effect on the mind, character or physical ability of an individual. And each level requires that parents have a different understanding of the challenges and difficulties facing their children. As such, Step 6 covers some of the basic rules for discipline.

Primary (or elementary) education consists of the first 5-7 years of formal, structured education. In general, education consists of six or eight years of schooling starting at the age of five or six. The division between primary and secondary education is somewhat arbitrary, but it generally occurs at about eleven or twelve years of age. Some education systems have separate middle schools, with the transition to the final stage of secondary education taking place at around the age of fourteen. Primary schools are often subdivided into pre-school and junior schools.

The first years of schooling can be very difficult for some children. First and foremost, they need to learn how to get along with their peers as well understand how to take directions from an adult (teacher) who is a stranger. They will need both your support and your discipline.

The exact boundary between primary and secondary education is generally around the seventh to the tenth year of schooling. Secondary education occurs mainly during the teenage years. The purpose of secondary education can be to provide common knowledge, to prepare for higher education or to train directly in a profession. Be aware that your children are undergoing sexual development and require constant supervision. It is especially important that you answer their questions as well as set a moral standard for them to observe.

Higher education, also called tertiary, third stage, or post secondary education, is the non-compulsory educational level that follows the completion of secondary education, such as a high school. Tertiary education is normally taken to include undergraduate and postgraduate education, as well as vocational education and training. Colleges and universities are the main institutions that provide tertiary education. For your children to really make advances in life, a college education is almost mandatory. Therefore start preparing your children early in life for advanced education by setting up a financial program to cover their college or vocational schooling years.

Step 4—Set an Example

Children learn by observing adults, particularly their parents. Make certain your behavior is role-model material. You'll make a much stronger impression by putting your own belongings away rather than just issuing orders to your child to pick up toys while your own belongings are left lying around. And role modeling doesn't mean that children should just observe, have them participate in projects with you. For example, my dad taught me how to fish and I participated with him in many other outdoor activities.

He was a store manager, and I often went there with him after hours. Later when I was a teenager, I worked at his store. As a result, I learned a lot about the retail business. I went to art classes with my son and later on with my grandson. When my son was a teenager, I had him help me with various construction projects around the house.

Mothers can have their children help in the kitchen, especially when baking a cake or cookies. The children can also help set the table at dinner time and help in the clean up afterwards. These events not only teach your children self-discipline, but provide quality time for you to bond with them.

Step 5—Discipline

Whatever your child's age, it's important to be consistent when it comes to discipline. If parents don't stick to the rules and consequences they set up, their children aren't likely to either. Equally important is to teach your children respect of others, as well as themselves.

But first, a word about spanking. Perhaps no form of discipline is more controversial than spanking. In fact, spanking a child is against the law in many countries. Here are some reasons why the American Academy of Pediatrics (AAP) discourages spanking:

- Spanking teaches children that it's OK to hit when they're angry.
- Spanking can physically harm a child.
- Rather than teaching children how to change their behavior, spanking makes them fearful of their parents and merely teaches them to avoid getting caught.
- For children seeking attention by acting out, spanking may inadvertently "reward" them—negative attention being better than no attention at all.

Learning how to effectively discipline your child is an important skill that all parents need to learn. Discipline is not the same as punishment. Instead, discipline involves teaching your child important items, such as right from wrong, respecting the rights of others and acceptable behavior. You should help the child feel secure, loved, self confident, self-disciplined, and know how to control his/her impulses. Equally important is helping the child to overcome frustration when stressed from difficult events either at school, at play or at home.

Remember that all children are different and have different temperaments and developmental levels. Therefore, discipline that works with other children may not work with yours. Thus, if you have difficulty disciplining your child, you may not be doing anything particularly wrong.

You should understand that how you behave when disciplining your child will help to determine how your child is going to behave or misbehave in the future. If you give in after your child repeatedly argues, becomes violent or has a temper tantrum, then he/she will learn to repeat this behavior because he/she knows you may eventually give in. Being firm and consistent teaches the child that it doesn't pay to avoid or fight doing what he/she is eventually going to have to do anyway. Some children, however, will feel like they won if they put off doing something that they didn't want to do for even a few minutes.

Maintain consistency in disciplining your child. It is normal for children to test their limits, and if you are inconsistent in setting the limits, then you will be encouraging further misbehavior. Therefore, stay calm and do not get carried away. Yelling and screaming at the child can teach him/her it is ok to lose control. Ensure that your child feels safe and secure and is loved.

Try to avoid too much criticism and don't overly praise your child. Be positive in your comments and remember to reward him/her when they do something especially good. Avoiding bribes to get them to do something they should have done anyway is the best policy.

A major problem is that discipline is lacking in many schools. Your child should understand that bullying is not acceptable. Playground bullies regard themselves as superior to other children and low self-esteem is usually found among the victims of bullies, but seldom among bullies themselves. Despite the fact that teasing is often considered to be the twin of bullying, research has shown that teasing can be a positive force in relationships. Friendly teasing is a form of play in families, and even parents can tease children to enjoy their interactions with them. It can even help people express affection in romantic relationships and improve likeability in groups.

Grade-school children know that happy, fun teasing can be an important part of play and can enhance their ability to express liking for one another. In other words, teasing can be a way of building and maintaining relationships, bringing up difficult topics, and just clowning around with friends. Teasing is a fascinating communication skill. Unlike bullying, which is a demonstration of aggression with harmful intentions, teasing allows a challenge to another person in a playful way. Teasing is a balancing act between a challenge to the needs and wants of another person, with the sense or message that the teaser is playing around. If the target of the tease does not understand the play, the tease is perceived in hurtful ways. If the target perceives the tease as playful, then it can continue. Teasing well, and taking teasing well, is a skill that adults can help children learn.

Step 6—Hobbies

I believe it is very important for children to have creative hobbies. When I was growing up, I lived by the Mississippi River. Pleasure boating was not really in vogue at that time, but several of my friend's parents had pleasure boats and I really wanted one of my own. Since I was a model airplane freak, my Dad told me that if I built a boat, he would buy a motor for it. Since I was an avid reader of *Mechanics Illustrated*, I found a boat plan for a 12 foot runabout that I felt I could handle. I built that boat mostly on my own while in the 9th grade, with minimal help from my Dad.

My wife's hobby was sewing. This allowed her to create many items for the house and to become quite a decorator. Hobbies can bring much pleasure to many children. They are defined as almost anything a person likes to do in their spare time. Some children like to spend their free time swimming, or playing some type of sports. Others have special talents like singing that they like to try and cultivate. A hobby offers a balance between work and play, and helps to prevent boredom. However worthwhile a hobby may be, it is important to estimate what the cost of this hobby will be. Set up a budget and stick with it. Keep in mind how you use your resources can really help. If in order to finance your child's hobby you have to get a part time job, then it is probably not worth it. At times serious hobbyists crave to be with others who enjoy the same pursuit. As a parent you will also want to keep in mind the type of attitude that this hobby encourages. Does it make your child a little too competitive?

Hobbies for children can be creative for parents as well. I like painting and I have taken both my son and then my grandson to painting classes. Since both were very talented, I took them to adult classes and they actually fit in quite well. Not only were they an inspiration to the adults, they actually enjoyed being treated as adults.

Step 7—Friends

It is very important for you to know just who your child's friends are. Parents can encourage their children to make friends by welcoming other children to their home and yard. When the children bring their friends home after school, a mother who is really glad to see them can make the other children feel that this is a fine place to come, a good place to play. Such hospitality gives security to a child, a feeling that his home belongs to him, too. Plenty of outdoor equipment stimulates wholesome play and brings a group together. Some good indoor games for rainy days will make the older children want to come over for a while. A picnic in the back yard on Saturday or popcorn around the fire on a cold afternoon may take a bit of planning, but they pay big dividends in helping children to be friendly.

From the time children are quite small they can help a mother prepare not only for their friends, but for hers, too. Entertaining should be a family pleasure, shared by all. Keep a well filled cookie jar and have drinks such as milk and fruit juices available for your child's friends.

The fact that the door is always open to your children's friends does not mean that they should be allowed to "run wild" through your house and yard. There should be simple rules about putting things away when the games are over. There should also be rules about running in the house and loud shouting. Some games are for out-of-doors. Your child can learn thoughtfulness for other people as they learn to be a good friend to others.

If a child has felt free to bring his friends home during his childhood years, the habit will usually carry over into adolescence, providing the older children feel free to invite their friends to the home. They might be allowed to even roll up the rugs and dance or even cook supper. When your children are in your home there is no worry as to where they are or what activities they are involved in, so it's well worth the effort to make their friends welcome in your home.

Sometimes your children also need to be able to meet your adult friends as well. If they have good friendships with adults when they are small, then they will know how to interact with adults as they grow older. Remember a child who has friends among both adults and children is well equipped to meet the social needs of his life.

Friendships with those of our own age, or with those of different ages, add immeasurably to the richness of life. Also as a parent there can be no deeper reward than knowing that your child has developed a fine, warm, friendly personality. The time which parents spend in helping their children have friends is time well-spent and adds to a child's personal traits, which will make them secure in winning the acceptance and affection of others.

Step 8—Baby Sitters

There are numerous articles in the newspapers about babysitters. Whether you need a babysitter or if one of your children is about to become a babysitter, they must understand that there are certain rules that must be followed. One of the prime concerns for selecting (or in the case of your own child being a babysitter) is safety for your child and of course, the sitter. Of course, the sitter must really love and care for children. As such, discipline may become an issue. There are many cases where parents have a hidden camera and sitters are shown beating and even molesting little children. Ensure that rules and regulations are established for both the child and the sitter.

Safety concerns should include what to do in the case of fire, medicines for the child, emergency phone numbers, the operation of appliances and any devices in the home. In addition, the babysitter should not have any friends over while he/she is working.

Step 9—Pets

Pets can be part of child's life. Parental involvement, open discussion, and planning are necessary to help make pet ownership a positive experience for everyone in the family. Children who learn the proper care for an animal, and treat it kindly and patiently, may get invaluable experience in learning to how to deal with people. Careless treatment of animals is unhealthy for both the pet and the child involved.

While all kinds of pets can bring children pleasure, it is important to choose a pet that is right for your family, your home, and your lifestyle; and one that your child can help care for. You should be cautious about having aggressive animals as pets. Also, exotic and unusual animals may be difficult to care for and really should not be considered.

There are many benefits to a child having a pet. Developing positive feelings about pets can contribute to a child's self-esteem and self-confidence. Positive relationships with pets can aid in the development of trusting relationships with others. A good relationship with a pet can also help in developing non-verbal communication, compassion, and empathy. Some rules or guidelines are necessary if children are to have pets. Younger children need to be monitored when interacting with pets and should understand that they cannot be angry or harmful with a pet. Older children need to understand that pets require specific care and that the pet requires as much love as any other member of the family.

Pets can serve different purposes for children. They can be safe recipients of secrets and private thoughts—children often talk to their pets, like they do their stuffed animals. Pets provide lessons about life; reproduction, birth, illnesses, accidents, death, and bereavement.

Although most children are gentle and appropriate with pets, some may be overly rough or even abusive. If such behavior persists, it may indicate your child has significant emotional problems. Any child who abuses, tortures or kills animals should be referred to a child psychiatrist for evaluation.

Step 10—Allowances and Cars

Children seem to learn about the facts of life very quickly. Unfortunately, they don't learn about the value of money as quickly. When establishing a child's allowance, one must also take into account his or her expenses. And the child will have different expenses at different stages. Therefore, you must teach them the value of money. Show them how money works. They see you swipe your credit or debit card, but have they seen how a bank works? Show them how when bills come in, a check is written and that the money comes out of your bank account. Or show them how some money is automatically taken out, such as with house payments, or how one can pay via a computer.

The main thing is to have them understand that there is no big hopper up in the sky that automatically shells out money whenever someone wants it. They need to understand that you have to work for it and that they will have to monitor their own expenses the same way you do. At some point, have them establish a savings account and see that their expenses come out from their own savings. Whether this account is funded by allowances or from their own work income or from a combination of both, help them understand how money works.

You may not believe in paying your child for doing household chores because when we were growing up, chores were a given, and our parents never would have paid us for doing simple things that contributed to the smooth running of the household. But that was also the era when we walked to school every day…and without a cell phone.

Today, things are different. Right or wrong, allowances are part of our culture. There is a big difference between mandatory chores your son or daughter should do just because he or she is part of the family, and the extra ones you might consider paying for.

Before you cringe at the thought of buying your children's services, look at it this way: You'll be teaching worthwhile lessons that will serve your child well into the future—a sense of responsibility, strong work ethic, and the knowledge that you value and appreciate their efforts.

So how do you decide which chores are obligatory and which ones are extras? First, mandatory tasks should be age-appropriate. They could include setting and/or clearing the table after meals, loading and unloading the dishwasher, keeping their rooms tidy, taking out the trash and recycling, sorting laundry into lights and darks, helping care for family pets, doing some babysitting for a younger sibling, and helping plan a meal now and then. As they get older, that list of responsibilities should grow as well. Children should understand that everyone in the family contributes to the best of his or her abilities without expecting to be paid for every single task. That's what families are all about.

Bigger jobs, tasks that take a lot more time than a daily to-do list, or projects that aren't strictly related to the day-to-day running of the home could be paid. These might include doing yard work, organizing the garage, painting a room, or cleaning the basement

Of course, these are just examples. Parents should sit down with their child and discuss which chores are obligatory and which ones they will be paid for. It's important that everyone take part in this negotiation process and that everyone's point of view gets taken into account. Some chores are non-negotiable, such as projects that involve a child's health and safety.

Payment should be based on what other children are receiving for similar tasks. Speak with other parents and see what they are paying their child, because you don't want to pay them too much or too little. If there are extremes among different parents, then pick an amount that is mid-point. If your child doesn't perform as expected, discuss the matter with him/ her. Basically, the rule is no work, no pay. This is an employer and employee program and teaches the child a valuable growing up lesson.

Allowances start when you child is old enough to understand money. However, driving a car is altogether different. Getting your child a driver's license can be a trying time, especially if the child wants his/her own car. Almost 3,000 teens die each year in car accidents involving teen drivers with another 250,000 teen drivers injured. Among teen drivers who had their own car or instant access to one, almost 25 percent were involved in accidents, while those that had limited access, only 10 percent were involved in accidents.

When your teen does drive, you must set down some very stringent rules. Two immediate rules are: no text messaging or cell phone usage while driving; and of course no drinking of alcoholic beverages. Period.

Chapter 4
Housing

A man's home may be his castle, but it should be his wife's palace as well.

It is important for every married couple to have privacy, and this often means having a place of their own. This could be an apartment, a rental home, or actually owning their home. However, furnishing a home can be overwhelming, especially if one has never thought about it before. Most people just out of school, and married, have not the faintest idea of where to begin. No matter where you end up, don't think of the place you live in as just a building, it is your home, so treat it as such. Far too often, a couple treats it as a just *a place to hang one's hat*. I don't watch TV that often, but when I do, one channel I enjoy is House & Garden TV(HGTV). Often shown is a couple who moves from a rented place into a new house. And far too often, the place they move from is a real disaster. It makes one wonder if the new place will become the same as their old living quarters.

I must say that in every place I have lived, I treated it as if I owned it. As a result, I learned a lot about the care required to keep a place respectable as well as the ins and outs of buying and moving. My dad was transferred several times and as a result, I lived in six different homes before going off to college, and since that time, I have lived in eighteen different places. Some were apartments, some were rentals, some were older homes and some were new. Each living place was a challenge, but treated as a home.

Step 1—Ownership

While ownership is desired by most couples, usually their first home is going to be a small, one bedroom apartment or a small older rental house. Just remember that this is your home. The main thing to do with this unit is to set aside areas for eating, working, sleeping and a comfortable seating area. Owning a house has many advantages for a couple…as long as they keep within their budget. Also, there are tax advantages.

Although ownership is desirable, it can present many problems to a couple. First and foremost is having an adequate understanding of the finances involved. Just paying all the items outside of the mortgage can be tremendous. There are taxes, utilities, maintenance costs, insurance, furnishings costs, and in some cases, homeowner fees just to name a few. And then there may be even hidden expenses such as liens.

For example, when I moved to Michigan from California, I thought I knew everything about buying a house. I had a real estate broker's license in California and was quite knowledgeable about housing in that state. However, I found out the hard way that a lien in Michigan is not treated the same as a lien in California. I was assured that there were no liens on the house I was purchasing. Was I ever wrong. There were two very big liens, one for road improvements and the other for sewers. However, they did not show up on the purchase agreement because, even though both had been approved, they hadn't been rolled over to the county clerk's desk. I did take the issue to the local court and did get some satisfaction, but not what I was really looking for.

Therefore, when buying, and even in some cases when renting, read that contract…and then read it again.

Step 2—Location—Location—Location

Most real estate sales people will tell you that the key to real estate is "Location—Location—Location". In other words, ensure that wherever you rent or buy, that its location will fit your overall needs. In other words, if you have children, don't locate next to a highway. If you have a large dog, don't live in a condo. However, in order to have a safe, secure location for your spouse and children, you may have a tenuous commuting situation. In California, I had at least a one hour or more commute. However, the area was most desirable and the commute worth it.

In particular, know just what zoning laws are applicable to your location. This also holds true for gated communities. Theoretically, the primary purpose of zoning is to segregate uses that are thought to be incompatible. However, in practice, zoning is used as a permitting system to prevent new development from harming existing residents or businesses. When zoning doesn't necessarily work in your favor, get neighbors together and go to the city hall. As an example, when we lived in California we lived two blocks from the beach. One block away from us was a commercial district and up the street from us on the corner was a bank. Now a bank is a relatively quiet business, so it really presented no problem. When they moved the banking business to a new location, a tire shop wanted to take over the corner location. Now a tire shop is a very noisy business. The entire neighborhood got together and went to our city's planning board with a petition, and we were able to prevent the tire shop from locating there.

Step 3—Style

Again, common sense should prevail. Building a colonial style house in a neighborhood of Spanish style homes just doesn't cut it. In addition, you need agreement with your spouse as to whether you want a one or two story home. In snow country, you probably want a two story house with a basement, while in a warmer climate a ranch with high ceilings is more desirable. The main reason is heating and cooling requirements. A two story is much more heat efficient, while a ranch with high ceilings is a cooler building.

Lot size also can make a big difference. While a large lot places distance between you and your neighbors, it also requires much more maintenance. Likewise, in warm climates, one has several growing seasons during the year, thus requiring even more exterior maintenance. And a large lot in snow country usually means a longer driveway to shovel. So if you and your spouse don't enjoy yard work, or other physically demanding work around the house, get a smaller house or a condo.

Many couples who live in the North want another house in a warmer climate to use as a vacation home during the winter. Too frequently, they forget about the upkeep required on two homes.

Step 4—Decorating

The décor you select for your home is as important as the style outside of the home. And decorating needn't be expensive. For example, your bedroom offers you a retreat from the stresses of everyday living. Make yours relaxing and refreshing with a splashy style by using wallpaper or else a lively paint on an accent wall. You don't necessarily need to paint the entire room.

Far too often, couples decorate without a thought as to the overall effect on the rest of the house. Divide your house into areas of need. Each room requires flooring materials, windows and wall treatments, lighting, furniture and in some cases, such as kitchens and bathrooms, utilities. When moving from one section of the country to another, keep in mind that colonial furniture from the North does not necessarily adapt to a tropical area such as Florida.

Step 5—Maintenance

Having a house is lot like owning a car. Without proper maintenance one will be plagued with problems. Maintenance requires cooperation from all members of the family. Even so, many couples argue over maintaining a home. I am fortunate because my engineering background enables me to maintain and repair almost any element in the house. My wife and I split household chores into two groups with her doing the inside cleaning, while I take care of the pool and outside work She does the laundry and I usually handle the cooking.

Large homes require a lot of maintenance and if it is over 2,400 square feet, the wife will probably require housekeeping or maid service. The same is true for a house with a large lot...it will probably require the services of a yard person. One system in the house that requires close scrutiny is the heating/cooling system. Filters need to be changed periodically and in some older systems, motors need to be lubricated. You may have a water-softening system or a swimming pool that requires the addition of chemicals. In older homes, a wood burning fireplace may require constant cleaning. The maintenance list is almost endless, but the main thing is to be aware of all the elements in your home that require maintenance. If you don't have the ability, keep a list of appropriate vendors who can help.

Step 6—Utilities

One of your biggest expenses will be the cost of utilities. Water, gas, electricity, etc. are expensive commodities these days and without closely watching the usage, can cause a lot of financial problems. Many areas of the country have high utility expenses. Both of us are very aware of our utility usage. If you have children, they too have to be conscious of utility costs. No excessive time in the shower, or leaving the refrigerator door open, etc.

Step 7—Safety

Physically impaired people really need to consider the safety aspects of their homes. This holds true for those with children and in some cases those with pets. However, all homeowners need to make a safety check on their homes. Do you have an adequate amount of fire alarms and do you check the batteries periodically? Do you have a fire extinguisher in the kitchen and the garage? Do bathrooms have keys available so you can unlock the door in case your child or a family member or guest locks themselves in and for some reason, cannot unlock the door. Often the key can be placed on the top of the exterior door sill, making it always available.

A good way to start a safety check is for you and your spouse to take a walk through the house and around the yard, looking for anything that could be considered hazardous. Two sets of eyes are better than one, plus a when woman looks at things, she has a different perspective than a man. Make a list of critical telephone numbers for police, fire departments, maintenance contractors for plumbing, appliances, heating systems, and any other service contractors that would be necessary in times of trouble. Place a copy of this list near each phone in the house or if you have a digital phone with a screen, key these numbers in.

Swimming pools are another matter. The water requires periodic testing for chemicals and there needs to be a safety fence to prevent toddlers from falling into the pool. To avoid having gas cans in the garage and to avoid stringing electrical cords outside, all of our outdoor maintenance power tools are battery powered. Just the convenience of not having to listen to the noise of gas engines nor having the inconvenience of power cords in wet grass, have made the cost of battery powered tools worthwhile.

Step 8—Weather

Almost every area of the country has some form of weather problem, from fires and earthquakes in the West, to freezing cold in the Northeast, and to hurricanes in the South and East. Whenever one rents or buys a house, there will be weather considerations. Adequate insulation is a priority and helps reduce heating and cooling expenses. The same holds true for weather stripping around doors and windows. Be prepared for power outages by having flashlights and candles in appropriate places. Also ensure that you have adequate insurance to cover any potential damage caused by flooding, wind or earthquakes.

For instance, we live in hurricane country, so we have built-in roll down window shutters as well as a full-house generator that will come on automatically if the power goes out. We have several tarps available in case the wind damages the roof. We have extra canned food and bottled water. Our garage has a portable support column that bolts the column against the door and is anchored to the floor and ceiling in case of serious wind conditions.

All family members should be instructed as to what to do in the case of bad weather. Years ago, a friend of mine almost lost his daughter during a tornado. When the tornado warning came, he got all members of his family into the basement. His younger daughter decided to go upstairs to watch the weather on TV when the tornado actually struck his house. He grabbed his daughter as she started up the stairs. Basically, he had a tug-of-war with the wind as it tried to suck his daughter up the stairs. Fortunately he won, but his complete house was blown away leaving just the foundation flooring and the basement.

Step 9—Think Green

Right now thinking green should be a family affair. Teach green to your children if they haven't already been indoctrinated about the subject at school. A "green" attitude by the entire family will save you money.

In this day and age, think green when buying, building or remodeling a home. This involves having your house environmentally friendly. Green building methods are gaining popularity and there are many benefits to homeowners who employ green techniques. Green building can be affordable. The best way to develop a green oriented house is to have it designed green right from the start. Use an architectural firm that specializes in green designed or environmentally friendly homes. Also check your local and state governments to see if they have rebate programs or rewards for going green. While these programs may help with funding your green home improvement projects, they will not necessarily pay all the expenses involved.

From solar heat to low water flush toilets, potential savings are available in many new green products. Solar heat is being used for heating swimming pools and water heaters. Solar cells harness the power of sunlight and convert it into electric power that can be used to run the electrical appliances in your home. With sunshine being free, its only cost is the investment in the solar cell array, and they are becoming more reasonable every day. Not only will a green house save you money in the long run, it may allow you a larger return of your house when or if you sell it.

Step 10—Remodeling

Many homeowners get themselves into a pickle when they remodel. Quite often they don't budget enough or they use an unscrupulous contractor. In most cases a reputable contractor can get started without up-front money. If the contactor wants money for materials, then pay for the materials yourself. Ensure that your spouse gets involved in the project, because most remodeling jobs will involve his/her input.

When remodeling, be sure to discuss with your spouse to exactly what it is that needs to be done. It helps if you make some sort of chart listing these items, or else have a drawing made of the project. Just remember, changes in plans can be costly, especially if you are using a contractor.

Also keep in mind that city permits are required for many home improvements. Jobs done without permits may be quite embarrassing when the time comes to sell your house.

Chapter 5

Finances

One of the least discussed and yet most important aspect of marriage is money. Without adequate financial planning your marriage can be assured of some very rocky days. Many elements of your financial planning may require the assistance of outside experts, especially in issues involving the law. Additionally, accurate records are a must. And in some cases, a bank safety deposit box is an absolute necessity.

Step 1—Wills and Trusts

Recently a friend of mine told me about his niece becoming a widow. What was disturbing is that the husband was in his forties, had a young son, but did not have insurance or a will. The home was in the husband's name, so the wife is now in quite a dilemma. She is facing probate and large legal expenses. In another case I know of, the aunt of a friend died without a will, and her estate was hung up in probate court for almost two years.

However, this does preclude preparing for our eventual mortality. Establish your will and/or trust immediately. Likewise, review these documents periodically as persons that you mention for inheritance may no longer be in any need, or heaven forbid, no longer be around. It is important that you understand the laws in the state you reside in. In some states the executor of your will/trust must reside in the same state. Also ensure that someone you trust knows where there is a copy of your will and/or trust. Likewise, there are different types of trusts as well.

Commonly heard of are the "Revocable Trust" and the "Irrevocable Trust". Basically, each one has certain benefits and in the case of Irrevocable Trust, several variations. And typically in most legal situations, one can have part of their estate covered by one type of trust, and part by another. Since each type of trust controls your assets or estate in a different manner, it is best to obtain legal assistance in developing your trust.

Along with all the morbid details, one must also think of any burial procedures you want to take place. Have you specified if you want to contribute you body to science, be cremated, or any other facts that are pertinent in the event of your demise?

Someone who dies without a will is said to die intestate, which is the condition of the estate of a person who dies owning property greater than the sum of his enforceable debts and funeral expenses without having made a valid will or other binding declaration. If a will or declaration has been made and only applies to part of the estate, the remaining estate forms what is called the "Intestate Estate". In some states, a hand written will is legal, but again, someone needs to know how and where to find it.

Death is not pleasant, but it does not mean that you should make it unduly unpleasant for those that survive you. Your spouse will have enough sadness, without having the task of making all the arrangements that will be necessary to fulfill your unknown desires. Make them known by establishing your will and/or trust immediately. Likewise, keep a copy of your trust and/or will in a bank safety deposit box.

Step 2—Income

Your income is the sum of all the wages, salaries, profits, interest payments, rents and other forms of earnings received in a given period of time such as in one year. Unfortunately we're not all millionaires, as living within your income is a problem many couples face. One of the hardest things to do is balance the budget. If both husband and wife are employed, decisions have to be made as to how the income is going to be spent. Does one use his or her salary for expenses and the other for savings? Is a joint account desirable or do you have separate accounts? Do you share salary information with one another?

Many questions and many potential answers. However, these are all issues that must be faced and resolved before there is harmony in the household. Just defining *yours, mine*, and *ours* can become quite an issue. If you have finances that should be placed in each of these three categories (for example, you have an inheritance and he/she has a savings account that was accumulated prior to the marriage, or if you have a checking account to which you both contributed), have an upfront conversation about those assets and what belongs to who. Respect these important delineations. Doing so will make your relationship stronger.

Where income really comes into play is if one spouse has to pay child support due to a previous marriage. Each state has a different set of rules for child support and it depends whether the support is based on gross or net income.

Gross income is defined as the parents' income from all sources, including wages and investments, with no deductions for taxes or other expenses. Non-wage benefits received from an employer might be counted as income as well as military housing allowances or the use of a company car for personal use.

Net income is defined as gross income minus federal and state income taxes, Social Security tax, Medicare tax, and health insurance. Some states allow other deductions, such as mandatory retirement contributions, obligations of support to other families (other than the family whose support is currently at issue), and payment of debts that were incurred during the marriage for the benefit of the family.

For those that are self-employed, determination of income may be quite complex. Usually reasonable business expenses may be deducted before determining net income, but unusually high business expenses and depreciation that artificially reduce income may be disallowed.

Hopefully, all income issues are resolved before marriage. And sad to say, hopefully all financial issues are spelled out before death, as per the example in Step 1 of this chapter. Throughout history, income growth has had a great impact on morality, society and the family. Hand-in-hand with income growth is the element of greed. Handle your income wisely, be charitable, and above all, be honest…especially with your partner or spouse.

Step 3—Credit and Banking

A person I know had a daughter in college just beginning her third year. The daughter was getting a college loan and required her father to co-sign for the loan. However, the father had run up debt with a bank and had problems with the bank's change in policy. The bank had raised his interest rate to an excessive amount, and the person had delayed payment in order to renegotiate the interest rate. He was successful in getting a much lower interest rate, but in the process, his credit rating fizzled and he was no longer valid as a co-signer. What it amounts to, is that you had better understand just how your bank works and what its credit policy is.

As evidenced in the 2008 financial meltdown, banks are not necessarily all that cooperative even with their good customers, let alone those who are experiencing financial problems.

Step 4—Insurance

Insurance is one of those necessary evils that come up every time we have a close call in our car or at home or when our children come home from school saying that one of their friends had an operation. Whether it is car, home, health or life insurance, plan exactly for what you need and how much you can actually afford. Likewise, keep copies of these documents in your bank safety deposit box. Along with these documents, take photos of all items in your home and keep them in the safety deposit box as well. As I mentioned in Chapter 4, Step 8, a friend of mine lost everything in a tornado. Without photo references, he had a very difficult time when reporting his losses to the insurance company.

Another insurance issue is the amount of life insurance to carry. Life insurance may be divided into two basic classes—temporary (or term) and permanent. Term assurance provides for life insurance coverage for a specified term of years for a specified premium. It should be noted that such a policy does not accumulate cash value. Some term policies are for specific events, such as accident insurance purchased by you when traveling.

Permanent life insurance remains in force until the policy matures, unless the owner fails to pay the premium when due. This policy cannot be cancelled by the insurer for any reason except fraud in the application, and that cancellation must occur within a period of time defined by law (usually two years). Permanent insurance builds a cash value that reduces the amount at risk to the insurance company and thus the insurance expense over time. This means that a policy with a million dollar face value can be relatively expensive for a 70 year old. The owner can access the money in the cash value by withdrawing money, borrowing the cash value, or surrendering the policy and receiving the surrender value.

As many of us already have, health insurance is for medical expenses. Sometimes it includes disability or long-term nursing or custodial care needs that may be provided through a government-sponsored social insurance program, or from private insurance companies. Health insurance may be purchased on a group basis or by individual consumers. In each case, the covered groups or individuals pay premiums to help protect themselves from high or unexpected healthcare expenses. Social welfare programs funded by the government also have benefits paying for medical expenses. The important factor is to know exactly what kind of policy you have and just what is covered.

Step 5—Shopping

Shopping seems to be the pastime of many Americans. "Shop until you drop" is all too common a phrase used by many. While there is no universal panacea to eliminate shopping, a key is to plan beforehand exactly what you need. Shopping should be a team effort. Your children need to be educated in the techniques of wise shopping as well.

Whenever you shop, the question is, "Do I pay cash or use my credit or debit card?" There are certain advantages to using credit cards. A credit card enables its holder to buy goods and services based on the user's promise to pay for these goods and services. The issuer of the card grants a line of credit to the user from which the user can borrow money for payment to a merchant or as a cash advance.

A credit card is different from a charge card, where a charge card requires the balance to be paid in full each month. In contrast, credit cards allow the consumers to 'revolve' their balance, at the cost of having interest charged.

A debit card provides an alternative payment method to cash when making purchases. Functionally, it can be called an electronic check, as the funds are withdrawn directly from either the user's bank account, or from the remaining balance on the card. Like credit cards, debit cards are used widely for telephone and Internet purchases, and unlike credit cards the funds are transferred from the user's bank account instead of having the user pay back at a later date. Debit cards can also allow for instant withdrawal of cash, acting as the ATM card for withdrawing cash and as a check guarantee card. Merchants often allow the user to obtain a certain cash amount back (as if the card was a check) along with the purchases.

For card users, the difference between a "debit card" and a "credit card" is that the debit card deducts the balance from a deposit account, like a checking account, whereas the credit card allows the consumer to spend money on credit to the issuing bank. In other words, a debit card uses the money you have and a credit card uses the money you don't have.

A potential problem with a debit card is that it requires a PIN number to complete the transaction. This is a number the user keys in during the purchase. If you forget your number, you have a problem. Likewise, in debit card theft, a thief can easily access your bank account.

While a credit card eliminates this problem, unusually high interest rates can be added to the cost of the purchase(s) if you don't pay within a set time period. The ideal situation is to be able to pay in full each month to avoid any interest charges.

Step 6—Loaning Money

A sure way to cause difficulties with a friend is to loan him/her some money. But how about when your child is grown up and is on his or her own and runs into a money problem? The problem arises, are you throwing good money after bad? There is no set answer, but be assured that no matter what you do, there will be problems unless you have thought about the issue thoroughly beforehand.

First of all, sit down with the person and review all of the financial issues at stake. If the person owns a home, have they thought about refinancing or taking a second loan? There is no set answer to loaning money.

Step 7—Borrowing Money

There comes a time when you really need some money for a down payment on a house, car, or to finance your children through college. Do you ask your parents, your spouse's parents, or some friend for help? Do you go to a bank or other lending institution? The thing you have to remember is that if either family or friend agrees to help, you definitely need to give them a signed legal note with the payment terms to show your sincerity in paying it back.

Step 8—Investments

Unless you have an in-depth background in financing, family investments should be a husband/wife affair that may or may not require an investment broker. An increase in income encourages higher investment, whereas a higher interest rate may discourage investment as it becomes more costly to borrow money.

Couples need to make investments so as to provide funds for retirement, a child's college education, or some other future expense.

Step 9—Taxes

As they say, "the only sure things in life are death and taxes". It always surprises me to learn that many who run for Congress also have a tax problem. One would think that those with a legal background would be smarter than to not pay their taxes. Many couples who have tax problems have never thought about the consequences incurred by not paying their taxes.

Special tax law provisions may help taxpayers and businesses recover financially from the impact of a disaster, especially when the federal government declares their location to be a major disaster area. Depending on the circumstances, the IRS may grant additional time to file returns and pay taxes. Both individuals and businesses in a federally declared disaster area can get a faster refund by claiming losses related to the disaster on the tax return for the previous year, usually by filing an amended return.

Overall, establish and keep good financial records, and pay all taxes on time. Whether you do your own taxes or use a tax accountant, keeping good records will prove to be invaluable.

Step 10—Refinancing

If your mortgage's interest rate is considerably higher than current levels, consider refinancing to lower your monthly payments. You can also pull out cash to make a major purchase or pay for some needed remodeling. Unless one has a lot of equity in their home, refinancing is not a real solution. Ask yourself how long you're going to stay in your home. Divide the cost of refinancing by 12 to find out how many months you need to stay put for a refinance to be monetarily worthwhile. Typically you need to stay put for at least three years and secure a rate at least one percent lower in order for refinancing to be beneficial.

Contact your current lender first if you've just purchased your home. With a recent appraisal on file, you may save closing costs and be able to move more quickly by working with the same mortgagor. Investigate online lenders as well. Pay attention to fees and closing costs, as with a first mortgage. These will include the cost of getting your house reappraised and may differ a great deal from one lender to another. Consider limiting the term to be no longer than what is left on your current mortgage, or you'll end up with much lower payments but an extended payment schedule.

Chapter 6
Work

Work can be very demanding of both members of the marriage, especially if each one has a position of some kind in a company or in the government. Work often provides many side benefits in addition to a salary...covering areas from health insurance to retirement programs.

Step 1—Employment
It amazes me how many couples have no concept as to what each one has to put up with at work, or in the case of a stay at home husband or wife, the problems and enjoyment they experience in caring for the home and family. Fortunately, both my wife and I have a good educational background that has always provided us with interesting jobs and adequate compensation. Both of us had similar vocations, so that we could advise and understand what each was experiencing. Because we were both marketing oriented and managed marketing programs at companies that manufactured similar products, we dealt with many of the same vendors and traveled to the same trade shows. In fact, we both got our advanced degrees at the same university and even team-taught several marketing classes in continuing education MBA programs.

The point being made is that you should know what your spouse does and the joys and the difficulties he/she experiences. In our case, there was admiration for the other's accomplishments and support for any difficulties or disappointments. If you are unhappy in your work, you will often bring that unhappiness home with you. Take time with your spouse to understand joys and problems with his/her job. Likewise, when you go home from work don't immediately lay your problems at your spouse's feet. Enjoy one another, and later on set aside some time to talk about the events of the day.

Step 2—Work Associates

Work associates can be a help or hindrance. If they unload their problems upon you or your spouse, in turn you or your spouse may carry these problems home at night. Some work associates may be quite talented and able to assist a couple outside of working hours during a home move or home project. However, if these associates work for you or your spouse, then there may be a multitude of work related problems. This is especially true if you or your spouse show favoritism to those that help him/her. If you supervise persons of the opposite sex, be sure that you don't get yourself in a compromising situation that could possibly cost you your job. Rumors run rampant in a company and the last thing one needs is to be the subject of a rumor. Remember, it is always important to know just who it is that you are dealing with at work.

Step 3—Company Travel

Company travel can be very demanding, especially on newlyweds and couples with young children. The important thing is to leave an itinerary of where you will be at all times. Likewise establish a calling time at either the beginning or end of each day. Establish procedures to follow in case of emergencies. Whether or not children are involved, try to bring gifts or some token indicating that you missed your spouse and family while you were away.

On the other end, try to avoid unloading problems to the one who travels. Usually business trips are much more hectic than one would think. It's not party, party, party. When traveling for a company, remember that they are the ones paying your salary and remember your manners, as that may influence the winning or losing of a business contract.

One job function I had was in charge of trade shows. Some of the people at work thought these shows were party time and when the show happened to be in the same city where the company was located, I recruited several of them to work the show. After spending eight hours standing in the booth and working the show and then entertaining potential customers at night, the response I got was, "Don't ever ask me to do that again." The gist of this story is that business and business travel is work, and not necessarily fun.

Step 4—Company Functions

Company functions may include picnics, some form of entertainment or Christmas parties. Sometimes the entire family is invited, and the employee should use discretion whether to bring his/her children. Whether you realize it or not, you are on display to the executives that run the company, your spouse's colleagues, and possibly those that work for your spouse. As such, mind your manners and be courteous to everyone. Don't rush to the food line, and only take a modest portion of food.

Company functions can become battle grounds, especially if alcoholic beverages are served. Again, be modest when alcoholic beverages are being served. If you can't hold you liquor, you will be the talk of the office during the next business day. Avoid political conversations and gossip.

Step 5—Changing Jobs

Changing jobs can be very difficult for the one making the change. With both spouses working, a problem arises when one is offered another job in a different locale. Does the other partner quit and look for work in that new locale or dose he/she stay put and wait until the other has established themselves in the new position.

The family also comes into play at this time. If the job involves a move, it could affect the children in school, especially if your child is a junior in high school and would have to face his/her senior year in a new town. It could require renting/selling your home and finding a new one. It may also mean a separation from your family for a period of time.

Likewise, a change in jobs can drastically affect any retirement program that you have with your departing company. If you do leave, ensure you leave on a high note as you may need assistance or references from your old company in the future.

Step 6—Stay at Home—Moms

What is interesting about stay at home moms is that many of them think their children would be happier if they worked, while only half of working moms think it is just reversed, the children would be happier if they stayed at home. Most stay at home moms work as hard as their counterparts do in business or governmental positions. Unfortunately, many are not appreciated as much as they should be.

World War II found many women entering the workforce out of necessity; women reassumed the caregiver position after the war, but, together with cultural shifts leading to the feminist movement and advances in birth control, their new-found sense of independence changed the traditional family structure. Some women opted to return to the care giver role. Others chose to pursue careers.

When a woman chooses to work outside of the home, alternative childcare may become a necessity. If childcare options are too costly, unavailable, or undesirable, the stay at home dad becomes a viable option, especially if the wife's position has considerable compensation and benefits.

Step 7—Stay at Home—Dads

A stay at home dad describes a father who is the main caregiver of the children and is the homemaker of the household. Stay at home dads have been seen in increasing numbers in Western culture since the late 20th century. Almost three percent of the nation's stay at home parents are fathers. This is triple the percentage from 1997, and has become consistently higher each year.

This is usually due to economic reasons, such as the woman having a higher paying job and/or better health insurance. However, it may also be that the man can work from home. Likewise, the dad may work a night shift and therefore can take care of the children during the day.

Fixed gender roles have become less prominent in the Western world in recent years, allowing men to make their own choice of career without regard to traditional gender-based roles. Some men who choose this role may do so because they enjoy being an active part of their children's lives, while in other families, the mother wants to pursue her career. Families vary widely in terms of how household chores are divided. Some retired males who marry a younger woman decide to become stay at home dads while their wives work because they want a "second chance" to watch a child grow up in a second or third marriage. Additionally, more career and lifestyle options are accepted and prevalent in Western society. There are also fewer restrictions on what constitutes a family.

As families have evolved, the practice of being a stay at home dad has become more common. In developed East Asian nations such as Japan and South Korea, this practice is less common and in some regions of the world the stay at home dad remains culturally unacceptable.

Still, many men struggle to find acceptance within the role of stay at home dad despite the many gains that have been made. Many worry about losing business. There is a common misconception that stay at home dads cannot get a job and therefore must rewrite the typical family roles, forcing the wife into the workforce. Carrying the financial burden and dealing with children's attachment to the dad can be difficult on a working mother.

The role of stay at home dad is difficult for men who feel as though they had no option. It is hard for these men to adapt from being a financial provider in the family to being a homemaker. One 2002 study suggested stay at home dads may face a higher risk of heart disease. The men who willingly choose to become a stay at home dad are much more satisfied with their role in the family.

The bond between father and child is just as important as the mother's in the overall social and emotional development of a child. There have been many studies that suggest the stay at home dad's role in a child's life and benefits of the stay at home dad is most important, especially during the first five years of a child's life. The father is more influential than the mother's in how the child learns to manage his or her body, navigate social circumstances, and play.

In a study that compared households with a stay at home dad and households with a stay at home mom, the study concluded that women were still able to form a strong bond with their children despite working full time outside of the home. Also, women working full time were often more engaged with their children on a day-to-day basis than their male counterparts. The study concluded that in a family with a stay at home dad arrangement, the maternal and paternal influences are equally strong. This contrasts with the more traditional family structure where the father works outside of the home and the mother stays home with the children. In this type of arrangement, the mother's influence is extremely strong, whereas the father's is relatively insignificant. The study found that both parents play an equal role in a child's development, but the stay at home dad arrangement is the most beneficial for the child.

The stay at home dad arrangement enables the mother to work without having to use a daycare or a nanny. This arrangement prevents the mother from having to deal with the stress of finding acceptable childcare, checking backgrounds, and paying for care. And it also ensures that the families' values are being upheld and instilled in the children. Free from the stress of childcare, working mothers are able to actively pursue their career. This allows for a more relaxed working environment for the mother and allows her to focus on her career. This extra income will allow for savings to be made for the children. Thus, she can advance her career and provide more money for the family.

It is becoming more important and more advantageous for men to establish fulfilling relationships with their children. They are beginning to value these relationships over financial gains. These stay at home dads, however, are not embarrassed of themselves or their roles. They know that they are fulfilling their role as primary caregiver. Later in life the father will serve as a close friend of the teenager, and later, as the children become young adults and begin raising families of their own, the father will be not only a good grandparent but a good source of advice as to how children should be raised.

Step 8—Avoiding Affairs

A workplace friendship with someone of the opposite sex can easily become a workplace romance, especially if they work in close proximity on a regular basis for extended periods of time. To avoid such an event, do not confide in or complain to this friend about your own personal relationship with your spouse. Basically, keep your distance and keep it professional. Avoid conversations whereby this friend tries to confide in you his/her own personal relationships.

Step 9—Continuing Education

Many companies offer continuing education programs for workers and scholarship programs for the children of workers at little or no cost. My wife got both her BS and MBA degrees through such programs. I also got my MBA through such a program. In both cases, the only expense involved was our time in the evenings.

Of course, even if your company doesn't offer such a program, continuing education can be important for you and your family's future. I got my professional engineering license by attending classes designed for passing the state test. Likewise, I got my real estate salesman and broker licenses the same way. It is a lot of work, but it greatly enhances your overall knowledge and job opportunities. And education is something that no one can take from you.

Continuing education is also a great way to bond with your partner or child or even with your grandchildren. As I mentioned in Chapter 3, I used to take my grandson to art and sculpturing classes at night school. I cannot describe how invaluable this time can be, because it was so rewarding to me.

One important thing to remember is that it can be very demanding on the person taking such courses. A partner should be very supportive of continuing education goals for his/her other half. Their success is also your success, so don't feel threatened by their actions. Because education can be very demanding on time and mental attitudes, both partners need to keep the romance alive. Never stop courting one another and be sure to compliment each other's success in school.

In my case, I always cooked the evening meals so that when she came home, we could enjoy dinner together, or when she got home from work, she could study. However, it is extremely satisfying to be able to see your partner finish a degree and go through graduation.

Step 10—Retirement Programs

Whether your retirement is through the company you work for, or through your own savings efforts, it is never too late to start saving. We all know that social security alone is not going to solve your financial needs when you retire.

Generally, a retirement plan refers to a pension granted upon retirement and is set up by employers, insurance companies, the government or other institutions such as employer associations or trade unions. Retirement pensions are typically in the form of a guaranteed annuity.

A pension created by an employer for the benefit of an employee is commonly referred to as an occupational or employer pension. Labor unions, the government, or other organizations may also fund pensions. Occupational pensions are a form of deferred compensation, usually advantageous to employee and employer for tax reasons. Many pensions also contain an insurance aspect, since they often will pay benefits to survivors or disabled beneficiaries, while annuity income insures against the risk of longevity.

For a couple, it is very important to establish just what to do upon retirement. Are you going to travel, move to a warmer climate, live with the children, etc.? Without proper foresight, retirement may become a horrific affair. Maybe one spouse has a health problem or without adequate planning, the couple has serious financial problems as many baby boomers are on the cusp of retirement without the ability to pay their basic living expenses with the money they will have coming in after retirement. This means most will be looking for jobs to compensate, or they will be looking for extensions of their current jobs past the time they had hoped to retire and enjoy their lives comfortably. Out of embarrassment, many of these people will state that they don't know what to do with themselves in retirement in order to justify why they are still working to make ends meet.

Other couples who have adequate funding will just drift along, not really enjoying the fact that they are retired. Perhaps one spouse is a golf fanatic, and the other spouse becomes a golf widow or widower. Since my wife or I do not play golf, we did do some planning many years before retirement. First and foremost, we love to travel. So we started worldwide travel some fifteen years before retiring and continue to do so. Upon retirement, we also started a small business that we both enjoy and one that we can do together. This business involves dealing with people in our community and as a result many have become friends. Since we both enjoy writing (we had co-authored a technical book as well as started a children's newspaper), we have again started writing. My wife's book was recently published. And as I mentioned earlier, I took art and sculpturing classes with my grandson and continue to paint in my spare time.

Chapter 7
Grooming

How one maintains their person is an important factor in a couple's relationship. Personal grooming is the art of cleaning, grooming, and maintaining parts of the body. This includes bathroom activities such as washing, cleaning, combing and styling the hair and also includes cosmetic care of the body, such as shaving and applying makeup. Couples spend a lot of time in the bathroom, unfortunately not always together. In newer homes, many have two sinks in the master bathroom, which allows more grooming together. As they say, "Cleanliness is next to Godliness". Grooming is something we also teach our children, and until they are old enough to appreciate good grooming, it behooves us to be patient with them.

Step 1—Bathe Together

In today's modern culture, bathing together is becoming quite acceptable. Many homes have showers for two as well as bathtubs that can handle two people at the same time. Togetherness in the bath (especially with a glass wine) provides a couple the intimacy that was almost impossible to achieve just a few years ago.

Step 2—Cleanliness

Cleanliness, or hygiene, refers to the set of practices associated with the preservation of health and healthy living. As a concept, hygiene refers to medical practices, but it can also relate to cleanliness and disease prevention practices required in most aspects of modern living. There is nothing that is most disheartening than to visit a couple who doesn't practice basic cleanliness, especially in the kitchen and bathroom.

Cleanliness is also important in raising children. They must be taught how to use a bathroom properly as well as using a public restroom. Teach them to always flush the toilet and then wash their hands after using any bathroom. Until your children are teenagers, it is always a good policy to take them into a public restroom. Not only can you supervise your child's cleanliness habits, but also see what kind of people might be lurking there.

Step 3—Clothing

They say that clothing reflects a person's character or "clothes make the man." They might say that the lack of clothing also reflects character as well, especially at the beach. Spouses should be aware that how they dress might also reflect upon another's opinion of your mate. Dressing inappropriately when you and your husband dine out with one of his business associates is not recommended.

Step 4—Teeth

There is nothing like having a beautiful smile. Unfortunately, many children never had proper dental work and grew up with crooked and/or missing teeth. For adults, this can end up with what is often a painful and expensive corrective process. Therefore, ensure that your children practice taking good care of their teeth.

Step 5—Hair and Nails

Let's be realistic about it, women are probably more concerned about their hair than men. So it behooves a man to compliment his spouse on how special her hair looks. Because of the variety of hair styles, the most important thing is to keep your hair clean. Likewise, keep your nails clean as well.

Step 6—Body Functions

While we don't often talk about body functions, they are an important part of our daily life. Your children especially need to know proper elimination habits and cleanliness around the private parts. Proper digestion and elimination are vital to the health of the human body. These functions, along with proper absorption of nutrients, allow maximum utilization of food as fuel. Whether any one, or all of these functions, is impaired, imbalance can occur in the body and mind, which may lead to various health problems and illnesses.

Step 7—Cosmetic Surgery

Women in particular are very concerned about the benefits they can receive from plastic surgery. However, this kind of surgery will not necessarily improve a spouse's disposition. But then again, it may require a whole new outlook by the recipient. My son had been hit in the nose during a ball game. Unfortunately, he was too young for cosmetic surgery and had to live with his crooked nose for several years. When he reached the proper age, the crookedness was corrected by surgery and his resulting comment was worth the expense, "Dad, I can now look at someone straight on."

Step 8—Manners

When I was growing up, my mother insisted that my brother, sisters and I have good manners. She often read to us Emily Post's book on good manners. Good manners were also demanded in the schools I attended. Teachers wore suits, were addressed by their last names and were shown respect. There was none of this casual dress and first name basis that is used by many schools today.

Actually manners are the unenforced standards of conduct which show that you are proper, polite, and refined. They are like laws in that they set a standard for human behavior, however unlike laws, there is no formal system for punishing transgressions, other than social disapproval. They are a kind of norm. However, manners are susceptible to change with time, geographical location, social stratum, occasion, and other factors. That manners matter is evidenced by the fact that many books have been written on the subject. Advice columns, such as *Dear Abby*, frequently deal with questions of mannerly behavior. A lady is a term frequently used for a woman who follows proper manners; the term gentleman is used as a male counterpart.

To present a good impression, it is important to act like you weren't raised in a barn! It is difficult dealing with those having no manners or concern for others. A huge societal issue is a general lack of respect for what has been taught in history regarding human concern and compassion towards acquaintances.

"Good Manners" are an increasingly archaic school of thought that displays respect, care, and consideration. Everyone has a basic right to help another and feel positive about themselves and others around them. If you don't have an etiquette resource, consider picking up one of many etiquette books. Also learn from real-world examples—study the positive effects of those displaying good manners and how people react to and around them. It's common sense that people generally prefer a reasonable amount of respect.

Step 9—Living With a Weight Problem

Weight issues are a problem with a large percentage of Americans; 63 percent are overweight. The solution would appear to be easy; eat less and exercise more. But because we have become a food driven society and laissez faire about exercise, we have developed an attitude of being overweight…but not happy. We drive everywhere, eat and drink far more than we should, and avoid any form of physical effort. Persons in many foreign countries do not have our problem because they walk more and eat less. Part of the reason for this is the high cost associated with cars, and the close proximity of everything in their cities that allows them to walk.

If we don't care about our own wellbeing, how can we care about our own children being obese? Child obesity rates are skyrocketing. Our poor eating habits and exercising are being directly transferred to our children. Not only do we stuff them with junk food, but we allow them to spend hour after hour in front of computer monitors, television screens and video gaming devices instead of being made to participate in regular physical activities.

Be aware that along with the health issues that were once thought to be reserved for adults, an alarming number of children and young adults are developing completely preventable diseases as a result of our lack of controlling their eating and exercise habits.

But these are not the only weight issues we face. Weight issues become a real problem when only one spouse is overweight. Likewise, when our children are overweight and we're not, it can become a very emotional when confronting them with the weight issue. First and foremost, if your spouse and children have weight problems, they need support and not undue criticism. If you snack at night, they are going to join you. If you don't exercise, they won't.

The solution isn't easy. It requires hard measures from all parties involved. Weight doesn't come off easy and it doesn't come off fast. It requires a permanent change in eating and exercising patterns. In Chapter 10, I mention the exercise regimen that my wife and I follow. While we were doing to it to tone our bodies and lose a few pounds, it took over one month before we each lost a single pound.

Step 10—Personalities

Respect your spouse's personality as well as your children's. Personality is a collection of emotional, thought, and behavioral patterns unique to a person that is consistent over time. As such, we all have different personalities. The idea that we can understand ourselves and others by categorizing the ways in which we experience, respond, and behave toward the physical and social world has a long tradition. There is the concept of personality type, which refers to the psychological classification of different types of individuals. Then we have the concept of personality traits, which come in different levels or degrees. Types involve qualitative differences between people, whereas traits involve quantitative differences. According to type theories, for example, introverts and extroverts are two fundamentally different categories of people. According to trait theories, introversion and extroversion are part of a continuous dimension, with many people in the middle.

With the advent of psychology as an academic discipline, theories of personality and techniques for measuring personality characteristics and individual differences have developed significantly. No single model is able to describe the totality of human personality. Thus understanding and appreciating the differences among our own family members allows us to better communicate and get along with one another. In other words, let each member fulfill his or her own potential and yet contribute to the rest of the family, according to their own unique nature.

Chapter 8
Friends and Associates

Having the right friends can bring a lot of joy into a marriage. Unfortunately, many men and women select some friends that overindulge in bad habits, which in turn can bring much discourse into their marriage. Together, talk about your time away from together activities, like he wants to bowl with the guys and you want to play bridge with your friends. Actually, it is very important that the two of you are able to have a lot of fun together or with your friends.

Opposite sex friendships are tricky and can often be a direct threat to the relationship you have with your spouse, but they don't have to be. For most people, fear comes not from the friendship, but in keeping the friendship platonic, which can be difficult given that 90 percent of the time one of the individuals may have experienced romantic feelings for the friend. Sometimes this is talked about and sometimes it isn't, but the feelings may be there.

But limiting your friendships with the opposite sex once you're in a committed relationship doesn't allow you the richness and perspective that we can gain from a member of the opposite sex. With some foresight and consciousness, it's possible to have friends of the opposite sex and keep your love relationship with your spouse strong and healthy. As such, some rules need to be established to eliminate the possibility of conflict. If your spouse is out of town, getting together to party with a friend of the opposite sex is not too wise. However, if you have tickets for a play or other form of entertainment and intend to go with another couple, then having your spouse go with a friend of the opposite sex because you are unable to, will probably work. At all times, you must think of how any friendly relationship with a member of the opposite sex not only appears to your spouse, but to other friends of yours as well.

Step 1—His Friends

Male friends can be an important part of a man's life. These are men you can count on when the chips are down. However, male relationships can often be overpowering to a marriage. We often hear of golf widows, whereby the man is not only playing golf all the time, but drinking and carousing with his buddies as well. Also, practical jokes among men do not really set well with women. Yet, friendship is considered one of the central human experiences Americans are thought to be suffering a loss in the quality and quantity of close friendships Twenty five percent of Americans have no close confidants, and surveys indicate the average total number of confidants per person has recently dropped from four to two.

Before the increased mobility and the industrialization of the 20th century, male friendships were much stronger. There wasn't a tremendous amount of interaction between men and women, so it was only natural that men bonded. However with mobility and industrialization came intense competition among men in the workplace and yet they had more leisure time. Because of this, men were caught up in sports and other entertainment activities…and male relationships were focused around these activities. Although some male activities involve couples, such as an evening at playing cards, most male bonding activities involve other men. Likewise, job mobility made it difficult for long term friendships in the workplace. While men have fewer friends than earlier times, the friends they do have are usually quite loyal. They accept their male friendships without being bothered by criticism of the friend by the spouse.

An area in male friendships where there are very strong emotional bonds is the military. Working primarily in life and death situations creates intense bonds and a true brotherhood. Soldiers will never leave a man behind and are willing to die to protect their comrades.

Step 2—Her Friends

Friendships with other women have the potential to either enrich a woman's life greatly or hurt her deeply. In your own relationship, does your spouse show an interest in meeting your friends? And does he follow it up with a plan, like sometimes hosting a low-key dinner party? Friends are an important part of your life, and his knowing them makes him more involved with you. He will have to deal with them at some point, so if he initiates it himself, allow him to do so.

During childhood, the main source of companionship for many women was their female friends. The situation changed when a boyfriend entered the picture. And it changed even more when the woman married. Many friendships became secondary and even dropped out of the picture.

After a while, a woman wants to renew that bond with other women, especially if she has children. She wants to gain back the part of herself that was lost when marriage or a boyfriend entered her life. However, a woman recognizes that not all of her relationships are meant to be close and usually knows that she should not share intimacy with everyone. Women are more expressive in their relationships with other women than men are with other men.

Step 3—Entertainment with friends

There are many things you can do with friends that can make life more enjoyable and entertaining. From playing cards to golf and other sport outings, to dining out, attending plays and concerts, there are many things that your friends and/or families can do together. When living in California, our neighborhood got together and held annual block parties. Basically we went to the city and got a permit to close our street to traffic. Everyone contributed some food and we had play activities for children. This was a great way to become better acquainted with your neighbors.

Of course there are "rules to abide by" when dealing with others. In California, one couple would pay for the other couple when dining out, and then the other couple would pay during the next dining event. In Florida, couples tend to go "Dutch". When alcohol is involved, the driver should refrain from drinking and be the designated driver. Basically, safety should always be of concern when dealing with friends. My wife is very good at noting the birthdays and anniversaries of friends and mails cards to them on these special events.

Your relationship with others should not take away the time you spend alone with your spouse. Each partner needs to understand that friends can put a damper on your own relationship if too much time is spent with them. This is especially true if the wives are very close and the husbands are not (or visa versa). Therefore communication between husband and wife must be open and direct when organizing a get-together.

Step 4—Travel with friends

Traveling with friends can be fun and entertaining. It can also deteriorate into a visit into hell. My parents first and only trip to Europe was with their special friends. All expenses were shared, except my father's friend said he wanted to do all the driving. As such, they always had to go where he wanted to go. To top it off, my father's friend dropped them off a small countryside hotel, while the friend and wife took several days of visiting "their own" special friends. Needless-to-say, my parents were stuck in a small community where they didn't know anyone and didn't know the language either. As such, the trip was a disaster and my folks never wanted to travel overseas again.

My wife and I love to travel, especially overseas. We have found that traveling in a tour group or on a river cruise, allow us to find new and exciting friends. All it involves is being able to converse with others. Discussions can be about other places you have been, children, jobs, etc. Sooner or later, you will hit it off with another couple. And as a result, these travel friends have become permanent friends, and even though they live in different states and countries, we often exchange visits with them.

We also have found that staying at a "bed and breakfast" is another way to meet new friends. One advantage of traveling to meet new friends is that you can be selective. Are their habits and likes similar to yours? Do both men and women get along? And if disharmony develops, you never have to worry about seeing them again.

If you are going to travel with friends, discuss the elements of the trip before you start. If it is by car, who drives? What kind of hotels do you stay at, etc. Are they heavy eaters, heavy drinkers, and have other habits you don't particularly care for?

We have found that traveling in the United States with friends we met overseas especially rewarding. For example the couple, we met on a European river cruise, have been to our home several times and we have visited them as well.

Step 5—Family Gatherings

Your partner should ask about your family, and should really want to hear about them. Family interest shows that your spouse thinks about you as a whole person, and knows that being with you means understanding and accepting your relatives as well. Many of the rules for family gatherings would follow Step 3 in this chapter.

Holidays, graduations and weddings are just a few of the family gatherings we all attend. These events may be the main point of stress in your life because of possible negative personalities you may encounter. Families can be very sensitive about remembering important family dates or facts. We usually take photos at family events and send participants copies.

Step 6—Class Reunions

Most couples attended different schools and therefore had different friends before marriage. Likewise, there may be high school romances that each do not know about. Therefore, when attending such events, forewarn your spouse about the individuals you are about to introduce, as they may turn out to be an embarrassment to you.

Step 7—Neither a Borrower or Lender Be

One way to possibly lose a friend is to borrow or to lend important items. If a large sum of money is involved, at least put it in writing if you decide to help him/her. Oftentimes, you or your friend may forget about the borrowed item, or the lending of money. If you borrow something, write yourself a note so you don't forget to return the item or money. If your friend forgets to return something, either remind them in a friendly way, or else forget it. Nothing will end your friendship as fast as constantly reminding someone about returning the item/money. In cases where money or expensive items are involved, be sure your spouse knows and agrees about it beforehand.

Step 8—Support During Difficult Times

Special friends may require special support during difficult times. This is especially true if the friend is going through a divorce or experiencing a critical illness. Try to be there for them as much as possible. Someday you may need the same support.

Step 9—Criticism

Criticize gently. Don't judge too harshly. If you criticize, do so in the same way you would want others to criticize you. Be kind and considerate.

Step 10—Communication

Many friendly relationships fail because of misunderstandings. Effective communication skills are necessary if your relationship is going to survive. If you suspect that your friend (or even yourself) is unhappy about something, do not ignore these feelings. Approach your friend and suggest an open discussion. You may be frustrated, angry, or hurt and they may be also, but always try to stay calm and reasonable. Your goal should be to resolve differences, and the only viable way of doing so is through open and direct communication.

Chapter 9

Entertainment

"All work and no play make Jack a dull boy" is an old saying that still applies today. A person needs entertainment to round out his/her personality, and I believe it should apply to your spouse and children as well. I was very fortunate as a child as both my parents taught me the joys of entertainment. My father took me hunting as well as taught me how to fish. Also I grew up in a small town and could walk almost everywhere. There were three movie theaters, and there was never a problem finding someone to go to the movies with you. Entertainment has changed drastically over the years, but what hasn't change is the influence it can have on you and your family.

Step 1—Travel

The first years of my life were spent in a small Midwestern town. I can still remember my first trip was to the Black Hills in South Dakota to see Mount Rushmore. Washington, Jefferson, and Lincoln faces were complete, and they had just finished Theodore Roosevelt's face. It was a sight that I will never forget, even though I was only four years old. Since that time I have traveled extensively throughout the United States and don't regret any of the trips. I really appreciate that my parents taught me how to travel and enjoyed every trip. If affordable, I feel it should be a major priority with families.

The point of this is to see as much as you can, because this is such a great country. My wife and I still travel extensively throughout the world and the United States and enjoy so many of its sights and sounds. I have been in all of the states, except two, and I expect to visit them shortly.

Step 2—Movies

When I was growing up, movies were the primary source of visual entertainment. As a teenager I was able venture out into other areas, such as plays and concerts, but movies were still king as far as entertainment was concerned. During WWII, an important part of going to the movies was seeing the news reel. This was about the only way one could really get the feel of the war. To show the impact movies had, I remember one news reel showing a snow covered statue of children holding hands and dancing in a circle at a bombed out museum in Russia. You can imagine how this brought back memories when I actually saw that same statue during a trip my wife and I made to Russia in 2008.

I still enjoy attending movies. Although the present quality of the movie graphics is greater than I could ever imagine as a child, unfortunately, many of the story lines keep sinking to new lows. This means that whatever movies your children are going to see require some kind of review by you beforehand. However, there are still enjoyable family films and as grandparents we have always enjoyed going to see a Disney movie with our grandchildren.

Step 3—Sports

Sports can be a great outlet for couples or a family. Sports can also bring a lot of tension into a family as well. If your child participates in sports, by all means try to attend the games. It will mean a lot if some family member is in the stands watching. In high school, I got my letter in both track and football. Unfortunately, none of my family members were able to attend any of the games or track meets, and I remember being greatly disappointed.

One can participate in sports or one can watch. Those who participate should bear in mind that besides being physically able, it takes training and dedication to become good in each particular sport. It can also be demanding on family and friends as well. Those who watch can be quite dedicated as well and just as demanding. Just remember, not everyone has the same interest in the same sports that you enjoy, so try not to neglect others in pursuit of your own pleasure.

Step 4—Television

Television is like the movies. Visually, it keeps getting better every year. Unfortunately, the story content keeps getting worse. Much entertainment money can be saved by having your TV hooked up to a DVD. Movies can be obtained at a much lower rate this way and popcorn and other treats made at home can be quite inexpensive.

Parents often rely on television to keep their children occupied. Unfortunately, children watch too much television and often the wrong programming. Experts recommend that children watch no more two hours a day and that they don't have a TV in their own rooms. Too much television may cause your child to be overweight due to the lack of exercise, and it even takes away time spent on doing school homework. Likewise, it causes a child to spend less time with family and friends.

You may become over involved with television as well. Like your child, limit television watching and be more selective in what you do watch. There are many good educational shows to watch and sometimes you may have to learn to watch them.

Step 5—Computers

The computer is a great device. I have been fortunate enough to see in my lifetime its development from something used only by technical people to becoming a requirement in schools. Via the internet, one can find tons of information on just about any subject imaginable. Unfortunately, the internet is also a place where one can find also find tons of material on any kind of filth imaginable.

We each have our own computers and in addition to being

entertainment devices, for us they are work devices. Many of the safeguards you place on your children watching television are the same safeguards you want if they use a computer. Basically, limit their time on the computer and don't allow them to have one in their room. Parental supervision is an absolute necessity.

Step 6—Vacations

Vacations are a great time for you and your spouse to rekindle the romance in your lives. They are also a great way to bond with your children. From visiting big cities such as New York to traveling to National Parks, there is an endless variety of places to go in America...and if your budget allows it, to the rest of the world as well. Planning your vacation in advance is really necessary...especially if you want to make it economical as well. It is also important that you allow time at the end of your vacation to unwind and catch up with your normal daily life.

Step 7—Library, Museums and Zoos

These forms of entertainment are extremely valuable to couples and their families. Low cost and yet mind stimulating, they can be a great source of knowledge for you and your children. In addition to the larger city museums, true treasures are often contained in the collections of small museums scattered around the country. There are some 198 million artifacts cared for by the 12,000 small museums and historical societies, which collectively hold the stories of our rich and diverse cultural heritage.

If time permits and if the history of any subject is within your realm of interest or expertise, you or your spouse may want apply as a docent (lecturer or tour guide in a museum or cathedral) at a local museum. It is a great way to study the history of some subject you love. Although you usually serve without pay, it allows one complete and free access to the museum facility.

Not enough can be said about access to the information offered in libraries. We are avid readers and visit our library on a weekly basis. Before I was in the fourth grade, I had a library card and was a frequent visitor to the library. And when I was a sixth grader, I read to the younger children in our school library. Even at that age, I found it was a rewarding experience.

Visiting a zoo can be rewarding to children and as well as adults. The joy and wonderment expressed by a child as he/she sees a lion, elephant or tiger for the first time is beyond description.

Step 8—Theme Parks

I can remember when both Disneyland in California and Disney World in Florida opened up. For quite a few years, I lived near Disneyland, and now I live close to Disneyworld. Although expensive, they are great sources of entertainment for children and adults alike. Usually there are several themed sections to explore in many of these parks, so one should start the day early. When taking children to theme parks, be sure to watch out for their physical as well as mental needs. Children tire after an all day adventure and are apt to be completely "wired" afterwards. So be patient with them. As in any large group gathering, keep an eye on your child, as they are apt to run off when you least notice it.

There is so much to do…and as they say, so little time. In all probability, you will need several days to take everything in, especially if you are visiting Orlando, Florida, where Disney World and Universal Studios are major attractions.

Step 9—Telephones and Cell Phones

The phone is another invention that is both a blessing and a curse. From a business point of view, I don't know how anyone communicated long distance before the phone. And anyone in business today now needs a cell phone and a laptop computer as well. But for family members, they sometimes can be a curse. Due to talking on a cell phone or text messaging while driving a car, accidents among teenagers are increasing tremendously.

Before allowing your child access to a cell phone, I would want to ensure that they were responsible and understood the consequences for improper usage. This includes talking or text messaging on the cell phone while driving the car or using it to access porn sites.

From a communication, emergency and security point of view, a cell phone is a good thing for a child to have. This is especially true if your teen is driving. However, ensure that your teen fully understands the consequences if they misuse the phone. It is also a good idea if they don't have internet access, instant messaging, or chat capabilities, as there are too many temptations for misuse.

The phone benefits to a pre-teen focus on the safety perspective, especially if they spend a lot of time in after school activities, or spend time with another parent on the weekends. It is also a convenience for the parent, for the parent can call their child if there's going to be a change in schedules. Be sure to set specific times and places when your child can use the phone, such as turn the phone off in church, in a theater, and at bedtime.

And while you are teaching your child cell phone manners, be sure you observe them as well. It is so annoying to have someone talking loudly on the phone while in a restaurant or in a meeting,. If you do get a call while entertaining friends try to keep the conversation low and short. Courtesy pays.

Step 10—Foreign Travel

Travelling the United States is great, but being able to travel the world is even more wonderful. When I was younger, travelling to both Mexico and Canada almost constituted being a world traveler. However, with the advent of jet aircraft, world travel is available to almost anyone.

We have traveled extensively and have been to almost 40 countries on 6 different continents. It seems like each trip was better than the one before and I imagine the next trip may be the best one yet. One thing that I do on trips is to take plenty of photographs. Upon return, I place them in an album with a full itinerary of where we went along with maps, ticket stubs, and in some cases examples of the currency of the country we visited. In this computer age, I am also using CDs to store photos from the trip, but I still find that looking through an album is very entertaining. The recall from documenting a trip is priceless as we often run into travelers who don't document, and they really don't have any idea of what they did on their trip.

One of the best gestures we notice in foreign travel is when a grandparent takes a graduating grandchild on a trip. Such events allow the development of a special bond between them. This is also true of families who travel abroad. However, I would be cautious about allowing children to travel to Europe alone or with peer groups, unless there is adequate adult supervision. When my son was in high school, some members of his class went to Europe on a skiing trip that was not well supervised. The comments afterwards had nothing to do with skiing, but were about the lack of getting booze and the many "extra-curricular activities" that had nothing to do with skiing.

One of our granddaughters is in a college nursing program and had the opportunity to travel to Italy and visit hospitals there. Because it was to be a learning experience with teacher supervision, we had no problem in paying her way as a treat. Her expressed joy upon her return made it worthwhile.

Chapter 10

Health—A Key to a Lasting Marriage

Health is very important to having a fruitful life as well as to a happy marriage. If you have children, you want them to experience good health as well. Good health allows a positive impact when applying the following steps.

Step 1—Yearly Physicals

It is surprising how many men are afraid to have a physical. Yet it is this physical that often warns one of any potential defects in your body system. Likewise, women need yearly physicals as well as men. From breast cancer to prostate cancer, there are many diseases lurking around the corner from us all.

Step 2—Hospice, Death and Funerals

Most young couples have not experienced the death of a family member or loved one. But it is an experience that we all have to face and it is best if couples understand the issues involved at this time. Not only does it affect family members mentally, but it can be physically trying as well. It is said that there are five stages to dying: denial, anger, bargaining, depression and acceptance. Therefore, one should understand that when dealing with a dying person, you may encounter your loved one in a variety of moods.

At any time during a life-limiting illness, it's appropriate to discuss all of a patient's care options, including hospice. By law the decision belongs to the patient. Most hospices accept patients who have a life-expectancy of six months or less and who are referred by their personal physician. If the patient's condition improves and the disease seems to be in remission, patients can be discharged from hospice and returned to the appropriate therapy, or else return to their normal life. Once a patient is discharged, but later on requires a need to return to hospice care, Medicare and most private insurances will allow additional coverage for this requirement.

Growing from a volunteer-led movement to improved care for people dying alone, isolated, or in hospitals, hospice has become a significant part of the health care system. In 2005 more than one million individuals and their families received hospice care. Hospice is the only Medicare benefit that includes pharmaceuticals, medical equipment, 24/7 access to care and support. Hospice care is also covered by Medicaid and many private insurance plans. While most hospice care is delivered at home, it is also available in home-like hospice residences, nursing homes, assisted living facilities, veterans' facilities, hospitals, and prisons. As of 2008, approximately 900,000 people in the United States were utilizing hospice every year, with more than one-third of dying Americans utilizing the service.

A funeral ceremony is often difficult for family members. Children in particular can be baffled by what is taking place, and often require explanations of the process. Funerary customs comprise the complex of beliefs and practices used by a culture to remember the dead, from the funeral itself, to various monuments, prayers, and rituals undertaken in their honor. These customs vary widely between cultures, and between religious affiliations within cultures. In some cultures the dead are venerated, or commonly called ancestor worship.

Funeral rites are as old as the human culture itself, predating modern man, to at least 300,000 years ago. For example, in many sites in Europe and the Near East, Neanderthal skeletons have been discovered with a characteristic layer of pollen, which suggests that Neanderthals buried the dead with gifts of flowers. This has been interpreted as suggesting that Neanderthals believed in an afterlife.

Step 3—Sickness

Telling your spouse that you are ill is never easy and many people try to hide illness unless they are really incapacitated. You know a spouse really cares when he/she can't stay away, even when you're bedridden or moody. You may be sick or recently received bad news about your job, a family member or another friend, or you just have the blues. This is the time to bend over backwards and take care of the spouse. When you're sick, they want to take care of you. But informing family members shouldn't stop with just the spouse, especially if the sickness is really serious...such as cancer.

Your children need to know if one parent is really ill and what the consequences are. Granted, you don't need to go into graphic details. But if your child is old enough and wants to know, tell them or get the appropriate literature for them to read.

Step 4—Exercise

A person really needs exercise to keep the body fit and trim and to stay healthy. Both spouses need to be serious about this though and there are many exercises that the two of you can participate in together. For example, my wife and I exercise together first thing in the morning. We use Leslie Sansone's 3 mile power walk DVD just before breakfast. Basically it is walking in place and takes very little space. However, it does firm up the body and we even had a little weight loss because of it. We also use her DVD when we travel as most places now have DVD players. Another exercise we do together is riding our bicycles. We try to get out three or four times a week and journey about the neighborhood. Other exercises and sports that couples can participate in together include golf, tennis, swimming, and for those up north there are a host of winter activities.

Don't forget the children. Make sure they exercise and participate in sporting activities and by all means, try to attend some of their games. And boys don't have to play contact sports like football, although I did. However, I did get smacked around a bit because I didn't weigh that much. Soccer is quite popular for children of all ages, and we have enjoyed attending our grandchildren's games.

Step 5—Sleep

Both spouses need an appropriate amount of sleep. Getting a good night's sleep is essential to feeling refreshed and alert during the next day. Unfortunately, not all couples can sleep together as one either snores, or tosses and turns, or is up and out of bed frequently.

Seven to nine hours of sleep for adults is necessary for overall health benefits, as well as to reduce the risk of accidents. A cognitive performance declines with six or fewer hours of sleep. Studies also show that sleeping more than 7 to 8 hours per day has been consistently associated with increased mortality, although the cause is probably other factors such as depression and socioeconomic status. It has been suggested that the correlation between fewer sleep hours and reduced morbidity only occurs with those who awaken naturally, rather than those who use an alarm. Furthermore, sleep difficulties are often closely associated with psychiatric disorders such as depression, alcoholism, and bipolar disorder. Up to 90 percent of adults with depression are found to have sleep difficulties.

Sleep problems will eventually disrupt your work, family and personal relationships. There are more than 70 types of sleep disorders that can affect you and your family. The most common include chronic insomnia, sleep apnea, restless legs syndrome (RLS) and narcolepsy. A lack of quality sleep can cause accidents, affect your family relationships, your health, and mental prowess; and in general make you wake up feeling tired. You may muddle through your days lacking energy and feeling disconnected from the world. If that is how an adult can feel, think of what a sleeping disorder can do to your child. If you, your spouse or your children have a sleeping problem, it may indicate not only a sleeping disorder but some other medical problem. As such it is probably best not to try and diagnose it yourself, but to see your family doctor.

Step 6—Medications

Many spouses are on some form of medication. From blood pressure to bone loss to cholesterol, there seems to always be a short-coming of some substance or too much of another in our system that can be corrected by medication.

It is important to know that all medicines, both prescription and over-the-counter, have risks as well as benefits. Benefits are the helpful effects you get when you use them, such as lowering blood pressure, curing infection or relieving pain. The risks of medicines are the chances that something unwanted or unexpected could happen when you use them. Risks could be less serious things, such as an upset stomach, or more serious things, such as liver damage.

Because of the quantity of medicines we take, the medicine cabinet should always be under scrutiny. The worse thing that can happen is that your children can raid the cabinet and take medications that can cause them serious physical and mental problems. Therefore, either keep them locked as well as take a periodic inventory of the medicines you have. Are some missing? If they are, check your children immediately. Likewise, if they are acting strange, question them and if you can't determine what the problem is, seek immediate medical help.

Step 7—Over Indulgence (Smoking and Alcohol)

Most spouses who have smoking or drinking problems know that they have a problem and many will do nothing to correct it. Rather than lecture them, I like to give a personal example of just what it means to family members. My own parents were heavy smokers. When I was a youngster, there was always a layer of smoke in the house. We lived in Wisconsin and during the winter the house was essentially closed up from outside air, and the smoke layer became especially heavy. As a result, I usually had some lung oriented sickness, and missed at least 30 days of school each year. It wasn't until I went to college and lived in a relatively smoke-free atmosphere that I found out I didn't have to be sick during the winter. Although both of my parents lived fairly long lives, they both passed away from a smoke related illness. Needless-to-say, I am a non-smoker and so is my wife.

Around 90 percent of adults in the United States consume alcohol and close to one percent are alcoholics. The quantity, frequency and regularity of alcohol consumption required to develop alcoholism varies greatly from person to person. What is important for families to know is that those who consume alcohol at an early age, by age 16 or younger, are at a higher risk of alcohol dependence. Studies indicate that the proportion of men with alcohol dependence is higher than that of women, although women are more vulnerable to long-term consequences of alcoholism.

Step 8—Long Term Health Insurance

Many people feel uncomfortable about relying on their children for further support, and find that long-term care insurance would help cover out-of-pocket expenses. Without long-term care insurance, the cost of providing these services may quickly deplete savings if you have medical problems that Medicare or Medicaid does not cover.

Long-term care insurance provides for the cost of long-term care beyond a predetermined period and covers care generally not covered by health insurance, Medicare, or Medicaid. Individuals who require long-term care are generally not sick in the traditional sense, but instead, are unable to perform the basic activities of daily living such as dressing, bathing, eating, toileting, getting in and out of a bed or chair, and walking. Keep in mind that early (before age 65) onset of Alzheimer's and Parkinson's disease are rare but do occur.

Age is not a determining factor in needing long-term care. About 60 percent of individuals over age 65 will require at least some type of long-term care services during their lifetime. About 40 percent of those receiving long-term care today are between 18 and 64. Once a change of health occurs, you may no longer be able to purchase long-term care insurance.

Long-term care insurance generally covers home care, assisted living, adult daycare, respite care, hospice care, nursing home and Alzheimer's facilities. If home care coverage is purchased, long-term care insurance can pay for home care, often from the first day it is needed. It will pay for a visiting or live-in caregiver, companion, housekeeper, therapist or private duty nurse up to 7 days a week, 24 hours a day.

Step 9—Allergies

An allergy can be extremely upsetting to the sufferer. Family members need to understand and be aware of the difficulties that person a can experience.

Overreaction to the specific substance by immune process in the human body is better known as allergy or in other words, the adverse affect by any specific substance on the human body disturbing the immune system of the body generates allergies. An allergen, or allergy-causing substance, may not, in similar amounts and circumstances, react the same way with everyone.

Allergens can be airborne substances (pollens, dust, smoke), infectious agents (bacteria, fungi, parasites), foods (strawberries, chocolate, eggs), contactants (poison ivy, chemicals, dyes), or physical agents (light, heat, cold). The most common three are: pollen, dust mites and nuts. Like all living-beings these substances contain proteins that are responsible for causing reactions. Even typical drugs, such as penicillin, may cause an allergic reaction.

Most symptoms are usually mild although some are very serious, such that even death may occur. In America it is reported almost one in four has an allergy. The most common effects of allergies are: sneezing, wheezing, sinusitis, running nose, coughing, itchy eyes/ears/lips/throat or palate, a breathing disorder, vomiting or diarrhea, irritating body-itching and rashes or even some body swelling. Since allergies in children and infants are quite common, consult your doctor if such symptoms occur.

The best treatment of allergic reactions is to eliminate the offending substances from the affected person's environment. If this is not possible, desensitization is sometimes helpful. Antihistamine drugs may give temporary relief, but always check with your doctor first.

Step 10—Vaccinations

Most people have never experienced an epidemic such as many people did in the 1940s and 50s.

In the year 2009, the swine flu (H1N1) was an epidemic and possible pandemic. The World Health Organization dubbed the H1N1 influenza a "public health emergency of international concern." A global pandemic was predicted by various international organizations, even though both the seasonal flu and H1N1 had nearly identical national death rates. The 2008-2009 seasonal flu vaccine1 provided some protection against swine flu, particularly the most severe forms of the disease. The illness was considered generally mild, except in cases for people in higher risk groups, such as those with asthma, diabetes, obesity, heart disease, or who were pregnant or with a weakened immune system. In addition, even in people who were previously healthy, secondary infections, such as those caused by bacterial pneumonia or a relapse of the illness with worse symptoms, were considered very serious and required medical treatment.

These are just two cases of the value of vaccinations. What they show is that couples should seriously consider the various vaccinations available and ensure that they and their children are in tune with modern medical practices. My wife and I experienced the polio scare and both of us were vaccinated against polio.

Chapter 11
The Final Word

Even though some of the steps in this book may seem insignificant, each step presented contains a subject or issue that will be faced by a couple somewhere along the line. Whether you have children or not, you will undoubtedly face a child related issue sometime in your life. It may even be the son or daughter of a relative or friend, and how your treat that child may impact your life. Your likes and dislikes in each of the other steps will also impact your spouse or loved one, your relatives and your friends and work associates in either a positive or negative manner.

Sometimes the steps in your marriage or love life will take a step backwards or sideways. The thing to remember is that we all take missteps, so try to always be gracious, generous, and apologetic. In summary, be positive in your steps forward. Look behind only if it will help you in your forward movement.

In summary, you should look for the hidden beauty in your spouse. As an example, I believe my mother was a private person. There seemed to be an inner depth to her about life that I didn't realize. However, after she passed away we found the poem below among her things that she had written herself.

I walked in the garden, searching for light.
The plants stirred with radiance, but 'twas hid from my sight,
The sun shown with brilliance, the birds sang with glee,
But I walked alone, my soul could not see.

But now, after a weary day
I can lift up my eyes to the Lord and say,
Oh Lord, how I thank thee, for now I can see
Thy wondrous works seem all about me.

I have opened to Thee my head and my soul
With mercy and love, Thou hast made me whole.
For no more am I frightened, sad or forlorn
For Thou art with me, I am reborn.

To help yourself to understand just what steps you and your spouse are the weakest in, write down which ones concern both of you the most. Probably it will take time to resolve an issue of concern, but by looking at the list periodically, the two of you can overcome your problems and have a much more enjoyable life together.